Praise for S*c*

Following the tradition of the Jewish, Sufi, and Christian mystics, *Spiritual Wanderlust* speaks of our inner life as a wild love affair with the divine. Kelly has a gift for making deep truths edible. This book is a must-read for everyone who aches to live with meaning.
                                    – *Richard Rohr, author of* Falling Upward
                                              and Breathing Under Water

This book is easily read in a morning but its reflections could last a lifetime... This is a book not just to be read but an invitation to see where we turn up to the presence within.
    – *John M. Armstrong, Spiritual seeker and Catholic priest*

Every so often a book appears that makes you think, "Why has it taken so long for someone to write this?" I can think of huge piles of books I have read on the contemplative life, mostly written by "professionals," that is monks or nuns, or the classics, like *Cloud of Unknowing,* or the writings of Julian of Norwich. All these books are, of course, wonderful and inspiring and show the vistas of God, but what *Spiritual Wanderlust* does, is show you the ground immediately beneath your feet so you can take one step at a time. It is a deeply spiritual and mystical book, charting the experience of expansion, enlightenment, deep hunger, whatever you want to call it, and giving practical guidance in demystified language. I came across this book almost exactly a year after my own expansion experience and had I read it then, I would have been saved a great deal of confusion and suffering. This book is full of gentle counsel for those who find themselves in a powerful state of longing and hunger and who will appreciate the steady and compassionate wisdom that is within these pages. I highly recommend this book to you.

– Linda Richardson, artist, meditator, and mythical poet

A good spiritual autobiography is a key to open new mansions in the readers' self, inspiring them to plunge into their own quest with greater abandon. Kelly Deutsch achieves this in her profound yet airily written exploration of desire in her life - sharing what she has learned about what she (and all of us) really want. Her wide reading in the masters of prayer makes her see how carefully life has read her. So she creates a sense of personal adventure that makes any pain involved meaningful. Desire is her theme but her goal is a breaking through into the freedom of being, that is far beyond whatever can be imagined.

– Laurence Freeman OSB, Benedictine monk and Director of the World Community for Christian Meditation

A fascinating book. I read it in one sitting – I could not put it down! Kelly breached serious subjects in a playful, insightful way. I felt blessed having read it. Thank you!!

– Nancy A. Edwards, Nature lover and desert homesteader

Every now and then a writer emerges who is able to translate the yearnings of the human heart into words. I believe Kelly Deutsch is such a writer. As I read *Spiritual Wanderlust,* I felt myself not just resonating with her description of her own personal journey, but I delighted in

her phrases that capture eloquently some universal questions and her personal answers to the yearnings of the human heart. "The lack we feel is actually a capacity. Its dimensions hint at Who we are meant to receive there."
– Sister Mary Joan Smith, SCC, nautical nun
and wave crasher

What Indiana Jones is to adventure, Kelly is to spiritual rock climbing—no ropes.
– Audrey Geier, street musician, love addict, doula,
and possibly the author's best friend

Spiritual Wanderlust has a very intuitive perspective...The author has a gift with words that touched my heart and rang true with my soul, as well as practical applications to take us deeper in our journey. I could not put the book down once I started. Excellent book!
– Denny, an Amazon customer who is probably
too famous to leave his full name

Spiritual Wanderlust draws you into a candid conversation with a friend: one who wants nothing but your freedom and happiness. This book comes as a refreshing drink of water in a world - and a Church - that tends to ignore our deepest longings. Drawing amply on her own story, Kelly shows how experiences common to each of us actually serve as signposts to our destiny. Augustine and John of the Cross confirm what life has already taught this modern-day mystic: that your heart is made for More, and the More is closer than you think.
– Joseph Scholten, Catholic priest, desirer of the Infinite

A beautiful book that speaks to our deepest longings and what might be done to address them on this side of eternity. Using the genius of St. John of the Cross and St. Augustine, Kelly brings mystical words to us through the centuries to apply to our soul wounds that remain unchanged in our modern area. A wonderful introduction to the mystics for those not familiar with their works. A wonderful reminder for those who are. Kelly's voice ties this together with our modern day escapes and shows us the futility of looking for that which our soul so deeply desires in all the wrong places.

– Valerie VanMeter, lay contemplative,
dog rescuer, mother of millennials

In *Spiritual Wanderlust* Kelly Deutsch shares her quest for a meaningful connection with God with thoughtful insights from age old mystics. This may appear to be a little book but, as I entered in, I found myself inside a large volume of history and mystery that keeps inviting me back for contemplation. This small book will be on my bedside table to return to again and again.

- Liz Gauthier, pied piper, microactivist, and mother to many

Longing is such a powerful phenomenon and it's no doubt God-given. What we do with it---whether we befriend or ignore it---determines the kind of life we choose for ourselves. Let Kelly Deutsch guide us in exploring this inner realm and we may just discover along the way the hidden mystic in us all. A very engaging read that won't fail to stir our own heart and soul.

– Wil Hernandez, eternal quester and avid promoter of
anything Nouwen. Executive Director for CenterQuest.

Reading *Spiritual Wanderlust* is like walking up on a profound conversation between a small group of friends. In Kelly's case, the friends are St. John of the Cross and St. Augustine and herself, and in our case we are graciously invited in to share in the delight. Thank God for conversations like this! We need spiritual friends who have lived deeply--and are not afraid to tell about it.

> – *Stuart Higginbotham, dad, Episcopalian priest,*
> *author of Contemplation and Community:*
> *A Gathering of Fresh Voices for a Living Tradition*

After reading this book, my existential crisis culminating in becoming a crime fighting bat is now resolved. Yes, the ache is there, but now I know where it's leading me.

> – *Batman, dark knight of the soul, hope of middle-aged men,*
> *so "quoted" to see if anyone actually reads these things.*

As an atheist, I was pleasantly surprised to feel inspired by and connected to the words of ancient mystics. Thanks to Kelly's work, I now have a name to give to that Thing that unifies us all: the "I know not what."

> – *Emily Kerpelman, professional songwriter,*
> *life coach, dog enthusiast*

spiritual wanderlust

the field guide to deep desire

"Are not all lifelong friendships born at the moment when at last you meet another human being who has some inkling (but faint and uncertain even in the best) of that something which you were born desiring… All the things that have ever deeply possessed your soul have been but hints of it – tantalizing glimpses, promises never quite fulfilled, echoes that died away just as they caught your ear. But if it should really become manifest – if there ever came an echo that did not die away but swelled into the sound itself – you would know it. Beyond all possibility of doubt you would say 'Here at last is the thing I was made for.' We cannot tell each other about it. It is the secret signature of each soul, the incommunicable and unappeasable want, the thing we desired before we met our wives or made our friends or chose our work, and which we shall still desire on our deathbeds, when the mind no longer knows wife or friend or work. While we are, this is. If we lose this, we lose all."

– C.S. Lewis

"It is precisely the truest joy that unleashes in us the healthy restlessness that leads us to be more demanding — to want a higher good, a deeper good — and at the same time to perceive ever more clearly that no finite thing can fill our heart...

We are pilgrims, heading for the heavenly homeland, toward that full and eternal good that nothing will be able to take away from us. This is not, then, about suffocating the longing that dwells in the heart of man, but about freeing it, so that it can reach its true height."

— *Pope Benedict XVI*

Contents

Foreword

I remember the first time I felt it. I was maybe eight years old, and Bruce Springsteen's anthem "Born to Run" came on the radio. At the end of the song as "the Boss" opened his rib cage and gave free reign to some kind of cosmic cry in his heart, something broke open inside me. I didn't even know what he was singing about, but lying in my bed with my head near the radio, it was as if a crack to the universe opened on my bedroom ceiling and something "ginormous" rumbled through my soul.

The music of Bruce Springsteen and U2 take up a large section in the soundtrack of my life. So it was a special treat for me when Springsteen inducted U2 into the Rock and Roll Hall of Fame in 2005. That night the Boss put his finger on what I first felt lying in bed almost thirty years earlier: "A great rock band," he said, "searches for the same kind of combustible force that fueled the expansion of the universe after the big bang. They want the earth to shake and spit fire, they want the sky to split apart and for God to pour out." Then he paused and said a bit sheepishly, "It's embarrassing to want so much and expect so much from music, except, sometimes it happens."

Yes. Sometimes it happens. Sometimes we hear a certain song or piece of music and it awakens something inexplicable at our core ... an ache, a burning, a throbbing, a yearning ... Beneath our rather surface-y contentment with the workaday world, beneath our desire to earn money and live until Friday, there's a much deeper desire, isn't there? We've all felt it. Indeed, that collective cry that arises from the depths of our humanity for something to fulfill us is what makes us human.

That hunger, that nostalgia, that longing can be awakened not only by a favorite song, but a favorite movie or poem, or through an encounter with the beauty of creation (type "double rainbow" into YouTube for a dramatic example of the latter). Sometimes it comes late at night when everything's quiet, we can't sleep, and we're all alone with the rhythm of our own breath and heartbeat. In those moments, if we're brave enough to feel it, we sense the desperation of our own poverty, our own need. We're made for something *more*. And that "something more" is missing. It eludes us. But whatever "it" is, *we want it*. And it hurts.

Few people talk or write honestly about this "ache" inside us. This is why I was immediately drawn to Kelly Deutsch's book. The way she unfolds our interior experience is so rich, so insightful, so revealing, it brought a lump to my throat. I found myself saying "YES—that's it!"

This is the kind of stuff that really changes lives—not just tickles intellects, but changes you interiorly. It is too important not to be shared.

Thank you, Kelly, for going for it. No one gets to these depths of the interior life without passing through painful trials and purifications. The world is desperately in need of people like you and books like this that can provide a map for the journey of desire. I, for one, feel like I have found a real sister in the journey.

Christopher West
Author of *Fill These Hearts:*
God, Sex, and the Universal Longing

Preface

This book was first conceived while I was pursuing a life of consecration in Rome. I was living with a religious community that allowed me to spend four hours a day in prayer. It was beautiful, refreshing silence. And also holy hell. (I mean that in the most reverent way possible.) Any life lived authentically feels like holy hell at times. It simply means you're being given the opportunity to grow. With lots of Italians. And pasta. Lots of pasta.

I grew a lot in my time in Rome. I thrived while rubbing elbows with students from all over the world, and was stunned by the architecture and culture and warm-hearted people. Then I stumbled on life's "accelerated program." We call that suffering.

After two years in Rome, my life turned on a dime. The community spent a month each summer in the Italian Alps. When we arrived that particular year,

I began to feel very strange. "Must be the altitude," some sister told me. Must be — except that three weeks later I was flown home in a wheelchair and proceeded to spend the next 18 months nearly bedridden. Apparently the Alps have powerful altitude.

Those 18 months were some of the hardest and best of my life. Even more difficult than the physical ailments was the emotional component of the experience. Hormones were off, sure, but I don't doubt there was more than that. Suffering has a way of cracking us open at our weakest points. It wasn't pretty.

My time of illness was the sabbatical I didn't know I needed. I read 100 books in a year. I spent long hours soaking in the silence of the South Dakota fields. (Untold depths emerge when you have nowhere to run.) Fundamental ideas were turned on their heads: who is God? What is prayer? What is holiness? Then, after I had been home for a year, I had another turnabout. In the course of a month, my former community decided to cut ties, I was diagnosed with cancer, and a good friend declared his desire to date me. New questions emerged about life and death, my path to consecrated life, and what the future would hold for me.

I cannot describe to you the enormity of this experience. I reeled as I tried to get my bearings. Found tentative equilibrium, then reeled again. It took me several years to feel fully myself. What emerged was myself, reborn.

I share this with you for the sake of context. The initial writing of this was in an academic setting in Rome. Its deep revision has been the fruit of six years' transformation. Funny enough, things are much grayer now. Not in the "there is no truth" kind of way, but the "truth is much deeper than you or I can presume to understand" kind of way. Black and white, while convenient, is not reality. It takes real courage to question the black and white. But we are much more complex and nuanced than "option A - option B". It is much more freeing to let go of the memorized answers and choose to live the questions.

I am still learning this. Relaxing into what is; not being threatened by someone's views that seem diametrically opposed to mine. There is something much more peaceful about accepting a person as they are, contradictions and all. In some ways, it is the same for ideas.

I recognize that this might sound challenging to some. It probably would have to me! The coach in me wants to gently ask: what are you so afraid of?

What if the deepest truths cannot be contained in human terms?

What if two seemingly contradictory things could both be true?

It takes some mental agility to be open to paradox. Yet when we cease grappling and begin resting, and *welcoming*, a new peace emerges. And freedom.

In revising this text, I spent significant time considering what terms to use. I wanted this to be a source of light and wisdom for people of all (or no) traditions. That includes my friends who are successful atheists, Catholic priests, and everything in between. Some terms from my Catholic upbringing had "baggage" that I didn't necessarily want to imply. Or, rather — were often constricting. When I say "God", I don't mean the old man sitting majestically on a throne. I mean the source of all beauty; I mean ineffable love; I mean the vast and spacious fabric of being that unites us all. When I say "he", I use it because I need some pronoun to use. But my favorite name comes from John of the Cross: the divine is the "I know not what." Unfortunately, saying "I know not what" every time you refer to the-source-of-all-beauty, ineffable-love, and the-vast-and-spacious-fabric-of-being

— is a bit cumbersome. And one hardly abbreviates something so boundless.

To those who feel me: take the religious terms in this context. I use the writings of two Catholic mystics whose language and environment is understandably "churchy." But the value of their insights remain. It is just as easy to be black and white within a religious tradition as it is when we are without it. We are easily turned off by language that doesn't fit our concept of the world. I invite you to turn down the volume on those alarms. (Which very suggestion may cause some to go on red alert!) I am not asking you to throw out your judgment. I am asking you to suspend it while you approach these ideas with curiosity. Review it, turn it around in your hands, sniff or taste it if you like. Try it on for size. If it doesn't fit, release it. If it does, even in a surprising or irritating way, I challenge you to remain with that invitation. You never know what gift may be hidden inside.

I wish for you a great flourishing on this road ahead. I send you my prayers, well-wishes, and trust that transformation will come at the time intended for you. Will it be mind-blowing? Perhaps. Uncover truths that feel like something you have always known? I hope so. Raise pesky questions that don't let you sleep at night? *Magari*, as the Italians say.

It might not be pretty, but it will be beautiful.

Kelly Deutsch, 2018

PART I. WHAT IS DESIRE?

1

Introducing two friends

"Longing in itself is a prayer of deep intimacy and intensity, longing for God is a love too deep for words."

– John Chrysostom

While revising this text for the seventh time, I hit a roadblock. Call it overthinking, low blood sugar, or perfectionism— but what I needed was space. Let my mind relax so my spirit had room to play. (They are not great playmates when Mind becomes bossy. Spirit will then go find somewhere else to play.)

I shelved the drafts and took a metaphorical walk for a few days. I let my tension dissolve and settled back into the earth. Over the course of the week, without realizing it, I began to write the text with my life. That which had stopped up within me began to flow out of my pores, and I was invited to be present to it, viscerally.

•

During my Tuesday morning break time, I stepped outside to take my usual walk and call my friend Audrey ("how's your morning been?"). The sun was bright and the breeze was playful, but something in me was not. I paused to check in with myself. What was prompting the urge to "phone a friend"? I sensed an unease. I gave myself a few moments to finger over the interior sensations. *Melancholy and restlessness*, I decided. Or, as I like to call it: a "funk" — and this one was begging to be resolved.

More running, Kelly? I gently chided myself. I had not realized I was in flight. Calling my best friend had become second nature. Changing gears, I did a turnabout and strode in the direction of my car. The heat inside relaxed my air-conditioned muscles, and I let myself unfold. "What's going on in there?" I prodded carefully. "Someone is feeling hopeless…"

I nabbed a printed Google map from the console and did what I tend to do when unsure of how to process: I wrote. I opened to internal dialogue. "Ah," I mused, eyes closed, "That's it. I want to be held. To know someone's got me." That's what this is. Identifying it made me feel a little less out of control.

Break time over, I folded up my paper and exited my makeshift sanctuary. I thoughtfully put one foot in front of the other as I wafted toward the building. Halfway there, I paused. Turning my face to the light, I stretched my hands far above my head. I took a slow, deep breath in, and let out the air.

Reset. Begin again.

The rest of the morning passed with the usual conveyor belt of items. Scheduled a few meetings. Checked in on a new hire. Made some data look pretty. Sent out a project update. By lunchtime I was mentally fatigued and ready for another break.

I drove home in the warmth of my sun-baked vehicle. Upon arriving, I heated up my leftover salmon and roasted cauliflower and took it to the back porch. I'd let the sun work its healing.

The bristling green pines thrust themselves up into the sky, lined up like seven-year-olds about to start their dance recital. The oaks behind them waved at me, like the older, taller children in the back, finding a friendly face in the dark crowd. I smiled. The trees are always on my side, I thought. *Will you guys pray for me?* I knew without thinking that this was a reasonable request. They chuckled and waved in response.

The July sun was warm on my face, the sky a smoky blue from the wild fires in far-off Canada. The neighbor's daycare kids squealed as they chased each other with the garden hose. One let out a delightful sound: pure, laughing joy. It reminded me of my god-son. Clear as glass chimes, or a Minnesota stream. The innocence of childhood, before we learn to filter our responses. Instead of self-censoring, these children had a direct experience of reality, and let us know exactly how they felt about it. Here, it was unrestrained joy. I decided that sound was one of my favorite in the world. And that there had to be more of that in heaven.

Interiorly I embraced the scene. With a sigh I released it back into the big, wide world. It didn't fix everything. On the contrary. It seemed to add its own tender longing to the chorus. But if the spaciousness had allowed my longings to grow, it also massaged those areas with a soothing balm. I gathered my dishes and waved goodbye to the trees. They danced in the sun.

Freedom is coming.

•

We are all afflicted by the same dis-ease. Though we each experience it differently, the root desire is the same. We are woefully incomplete, and we find a myriad of ways to work out that tension in us. If we are truly attentive to our inner stirrings, they will reveal the questions we all try to avoid. Isn't there something more? What is it all for? Will I ever feel safe, alive, enough? Even at our happiest—sitting on the back porch, talking with the trees and listening to heaven's laughter—we still know something is missing. We are never definitively happy.

This unnamable desire for "something more" is written into our spiritual DNA. The love, the success, the mountaintop experiences we have do little to quench our thirst. It actually may have the opposite effect: beauty sometimes make the longing more intense. (I was fine until the Milky Way arrested me in my tracks, or that film drew my emotions out of me, one exquisite thread at a time.) Where did this unnamed desire come from? What is its purpose? And, most importantly, what do I do with it when it aches?

I've called upon two good friends to share their experience and reflections.

Two Friends

Augustine is a bishop and rhetorician from fourth century Africa. His big Mediterranean heart is full of a fierce intensity. He never did anything by halves. If he was going to study, he was going to outshine all of his class and get noticed by all the important people of society. If he was going to love, he was going to pour himself out to any woman he could connect with. If he was going to pray, it was going to be with tears or jubilation. One can hear him groaning his desires from across the centuries. What he really wanted was to return home.

John, too, was a lover, though of a different sort. He was a 16th century monk whose life of prayer was a passionate romance. While Augustine wandered (I picture him as a rogue gardenhose, flipping and hurling and twirling, until he reigned in the intensity enough to streamline it in a single, chosen direction), John was fairly single-minded from the start. He knew he had to go through some "dark nights" to prepare for this divine embrace — but he knew the longing was a beckoning. Someone wanted to delight him, even more than he wanted it himself.

I call on these two as icons of desire. They knew both its torment and its ecstasy. Far from our images of stuffy, asexual clerics, these two men lived the real life. Their circumstances were not so different from our own. Questioning. Ambition. Climbing the career ladder. Falling in love. Feeling disjointed. Daily humdrum. Being the odd man out. The difference for them was that they did not run from the ache. Instead of numbing or stuffing, they relaxed into the longing. Once present to it, they could unfold and see what it revealed to them. And what they found was an answer that stretched their hearts to the capacity of the universe.

Mystics, icons, dead men they may be — but I want to underline their humanity. Mystics are not mystical because of some fairy dust or secret knowledge they acquired. They are mystical because they had the courage to wait in their desires for an encounter with Ineffable Love. I am convinced that mystics are far more common than we think. We pass them on the street and exchange a few words with them at the grocery store. Some may be religious leaders, but many are janitors, mothers, and businesspeople. You are not excluded from this group. We all have the capacity and invitation.

And it all starts with desire.

2

Existential Restlessness

I like to take walks in the summer evenings in South Dakota. The wind has died down (anyone from the upper Midwest knows the wind of which I speak!), and the sky's colors are gently turning from peach to passionfruit. The stillness causes my insides to melt into a pool of presence.

But the stillness is not always comfortable. As my insides melt like a popsicle, I find other things entombed in the ice. Disquiet. Murmurings from my past. As the barbs emerge from the melting ice, it takes grace and a few deep breaths to acknowledge and welcome them. Hello, old friend.

The pinks and oranges above me are sweet. Delicious. But on this evening, the beauty is less soothing and more indicative. It gently reveals my disquiet. I am restless within.

While I have ideas of what is emerging, I know the root. I know that running from the disquiet will not make it go away. Nor will stuffing it with distractions (music? new house project? phone a friend??). It's an infinite chasm. No matter how hard we try, we cannot bring enough truckloads to fill the Grand Canyon.

This, at its most basic, is the cosmic conundrum. We, itty bitty finite humans, on the third planet from the sun, in one of billions of galaxies, have within ourselves an infinite desire. We are animals who want to be like gods. To some, this may sound a bit exaggerated. Are we so important, in the grand scheme of things, that we would have such audacious aspirations?

Man in every culture and time period has grappled with this question. We build temples and seek love and conquer civilizations all in the attempt to find an answer. Yet none of these quench our existential thirst. It's never enough. If Dante finally married Beatrice, do you think he would be perfectly content for the rest of his life? If Napoleon had conquered just one more country, would he stop striving? If Mr. Moneybags had just one more vacation home, would he finally feel like he had "made it"?

Neither fame nor security nor romance has brought man the happiness for which he feels he is made. It always seems just beyond our reach. However: there are some who have gained wisdom. They speak hope and clarity into our muddled mess. Perhaps, they posit, these strivings and longings are only hints. They are not the end game; they are only signposts to where the real action is happening.

"What is it?" we ask, eyes lit with eagerness and desperation. "Where have you found your peace?" We chase after the mystics and gurus looking for a magic formula. Seeing their techniques and postures, we mimic them, hoping for life-changing results. Still illiterate, we make a science of examining the signs, unable to comprehend where they are leading us.

The master smiles warmly and tells us to "go within." There, in the heart's deepest center, is the place of encounter. There is where we find the root of all desire: the divine.

•

G.K. Chesterton once observed that "Every man who knocks at the door of a brothel is looking for God." This is the great lesson at the heart of all spiritual paths. The man after sexual excitement is not just scratching an itch, but is reaching out for connection, for infinite spaces where his spirit feels alive. Your co-worker may seek your bosses' attention not simply to show she is superior to everyone else, but because she is trying to convince herself that she is a valuable, lovable human person. The invitation is to learn to read these desires as signposts, and the delicate (or sometimes forceful) movements beneath them. When we follow them, they point us to the fundamental thirst that undergirds our being.

Highway signs are not usually a cause for celebration. Some murmurs of joy can be heard from the backseat when signs are passed on the road; they indicate the progress made, and can heighten our anticipation. Images of our hometown flash before our eyes while we are 200, 150, 100, 15 miles away: Aunt Jacky's rhubarb pie; laughing over at how terrible we all are at croquet; connecting with old friends at the downtown festival. But the sweet nostalgia cannot compare with the rejoicing at our arrival. When we emerge from our vehicle at dusk, stretch our legs, look to the front door, and see our loved ones coming to greet us, we can rest. We are home.

Desire serves the same purposes as those road-signs. By highlighting our progress, it gives us the hope of anticipation: "almost there!" Of course, that can also make us antsy, as long road trips are wont to do. (How much longer??) But by giving us glimpses of what home looks like, it reminds us of the joy and rest that await. We don't expect those billboards to *bring* the joy and the rest: they are just the promises. "Once you reach your final destination, this is what you'll experience." Rest. Peace. Exhilaration. Belonging.

·

Some of us were never taught how to deal with long stretches of road. We don't know what to do in the wait. We want to be home — *now*. As a quick fix, we reach for our drugs. Something has to take the edge off. How about an app? Constant busyness? Maybe fixing others' problems, or taking on their drama?

Many are frantic in the search for something, anything, that will silence that inner whisper. Ironically, an error in method only proves the equation. That is, misguided paths to happiness, while never quite fulfilling, only go to show that we all attempt to get there. We all want something more.

John and Augustine knew the conundrum. They also knew the answer. "Our hearts are restless until they rest in you," Augustine famously realized. John, the doctor of desire, moaned through his poetry for woe that he had not yet reached that union for which he longed. They knew, from a very real and visceral place, that our existential desire, this restlessness, defines who we are as human persons. Yet this begs the question: what is it, exactly, that we desire? And where did this desire come from?

3

What Do We Really Want?

I once was having dinner with my sister's family. She had three young children at the time, and my nephew, age four, was having none of his dinner. "I want something different!" he exclaimed. "Joseph, you need to try a bite." "No!" came the emphatic retort. "I want something DIFFERENT!" "Fine." My sister made a few suggestions. "You can have applesauce. Or some toast." His pitch was reaching for the upper decibels. "No! I want something *different*!" He squealed his last word. My sister was trying hard to keep her patience. Pausing, she looked at him with her best mom face. "What *do* you want?" "I... want... something... DIFFERENT!" He echoed himself until he was unconsolably crying.

How often we adults act in the same way. We really don't know what we want. Just: "not this". We may be surrounded by gifts— perhaps a warm home, or a loyal (if imperfect) family, or a job that challenges us. But instead of gratitude, we think, "I want something different!" I want a bigger house. I want a pool. I want less politics in the office. I want my spouse to perfectly love and care for me at all times. That would fix the anxiety I feel. Surely.

So we get the gorgeous home on an acreage, quit our job and find a new one, and decide to leave our partner. Does that fix it all? I have no doubt that sometimes, it "fixes" a good bit. Particularly when we were enduring toxic environments. However, leaving toxicity and less-than-ideal circumstances are only half of the equation. We are the other half.

When the anxiety persists even in a bigger home (oh, the mortgage!), the new job (did she really just go behind my back?), and the freedom of the single life (not so sure I like an empty home)— it becomes clear that the restlessness is not from a lack of exterior things. If this were the case, the life changes should calm the ache and reignite the spark in our eyes. Instead, in many cases, the restlessness deepens. Perhaps we feel deceived. "I thought this was it. I thought I would finally be happy." But trying to stuff an infinite hole with finite things only leads to frustration.

Augustine could relate.

What it is not: "Things"

Augustine wrote a whole book about misplaced desire. It was his autobiography, called *Confessions*. He recounted how time and again he turned to the world of beautiful things instead of Beauty itself. He was a talented young man with countless possibilities before him. A voracious learner, he soaked up the literature and law and sages of his day. His ambitions helped him scale the career ladder much more quickly than his peers. He loved the esteem and position that yielded him— and the feminine attention. At some point, however, Augustine realized that although each endeavor provided a great amount of pleasure, they also came with a sour aftertaste. He needed to peel away each of these ambitions to discover what he truly desired. He moaned: "In how many most petty and contemptible things is our curiosity daily tempted, and how often we give way, who can recount?"[1]

Augustine would struggle for most of his life to free himself from these "contemptible things" which distracted him from the source of all his desires. He did not have some pivotal conversion moment, after which everything was clear and easy. He *continued* to grapple. Which is precisely what makes him a model for us.

Augustine searched far and wide for the thing that would satisfy his restless heart. After many unsuccessful attempts, he made the discovery: the source was within him. His masterful eulogy-lament is worth reproducing:

> Too late I loved You, O Beauty ever ancient, yet ever new! Too late I loved You! And behold, You were within, and I abroad, and there I searched for You; deformed I, plunging amid those lovely forms, which You had made. You were with me, but I was not with You. Things held me far from You, which, unless they were in You, were not at all. You called, and shouted, and burst my deafness. You flashed, shone, and scattered my blindness. You breathed fragrances, and I drew in breath and I now sigh for You. I tasted, and now hunger and thirst. You touched me, and I burned for Your peace.[2]

In order to discover what his heart truly desired, Augustine had to let go of all else that kept him bound.

He had to *listen through* his more obvious desires in order to discover what was at their root. Don't we all have to do this, even on a smaller scale? Consider your own addiction: food, social media, pornography, your latest TV series. What is this a band-aid for? With what are you trying to cope? (Hint: it may lie deeper than you think.)

"Deny your desires and you will find what your heart really longs for."[3] What emerges if you resist the urge to that latte? How do you feel when you shut off your cell phone for a week? After the initial wave of anxiety, the deeper answer may range from loneliness to ineptitude to worthlessness. It's not comfortable in the least. But it reveals what we really want: feeling loved, capable, *alive*.

This showed up in a big, painful way for me as I was coming out of my time of illness. I had begun dating a very dear friend of mine, who accompanied me through this period as no one else could. While everyone else was busy trying to solve me like a puzzle or cheer up fatigue-girl, my then-boyfriend would simply be present with me. When I needed company, he would sit on the couch with me and read a book. When I needed to be held, he'd wrap me in his arms. When I needed space, he'd bow out and give me all the time I needed. In many ways, he loved me back to health.

At one point, it became clear to us that our relationship wasn't meant for the long haul. We both felt it, but had a hard time letting go of the person we cared about deeply. When we finally had the courage to step away from the relationship, so much in me wanted to cling. This man had become a symbol of comfort in the times when I needed it most. He'd seen me scream, cry, curse the heavens—and gently crack open my heart to be bathed by God. Though it may sound simplistic, he incarnated the tenderness of the divine to me.

As the months wore on after our breakup, I knew it wasn't just my former boyfriend that I desired. I wanted comfort; I wanted tenderness. I wanted that sweet familiarity and safety that comes with the package of life lived with another. The challenge, then, was to turn that cavity in me toward the One who could fill it, whether through human comfort or the deepening sense of acceptance.

Letting go is one of life's fundamental lessons. We let go of expectations, unfulfilled dreams, happy memories. I thought I was going to be a nun. Maybe you thought you were going to be a biological mother. Maybe you thought you'd have decades to spend with your daughter, seeing her grow up and conquer the world and blossom into her adult self. Maybe you thought you were a shoo-in for the big promotion you had been working your tail off for. Maybe you thought marriage was going to be romantic and fulfilling, because, hey, you two were *different*. We all have expectations we need to let go of when life doesn't pan out as we expect. As a wise man once said, "an expectation is just a pre-meditated resentment."

Another way of saying this: life is grieving. It is said grief has many stages: denial, anger, bargaining, depression, acceptance. There are times when we'll feel we're on a grief treadmill. Denial that this is happening to me. Anger when realization hits. Rationalizing, pleading, begging when we start to realize how much it hurts. Back to denial. A flare up of rage. Deep sorrow. And we slowly live our way into more and more acceptance.

The key to living into more acceptance for John and Augustine is to discover the "true" desire beneath. Without that discovery, it is very difficult to let go of our security blanket. Consider it an exchange — or better, a making room. This is true for the more mundane things, like our technology addictions. But it is also true — and I say this delicately — for the expectations and the dreams we put to rest. I am *not* talking about grieving the death of a loved one. While that is often the ultimate "letting go," it is not the context of which the mystics spoke. Instead, they refer to the attachments we have to our "stuff" and our plans.

For example: what was I looking for in the consecrated life? What were you looking for in your promotion or your ideal marriage? What is it we want when grasping for control or attention?

"God means to fill each of you with what is good; so cast out what is bad! If he wishes to fill you with honey and you are full of sour wine, where is the honey to go?"[4] The great Source of all Being desires your flourishing. Sometimes that involves letting go of our lesser vision for our life. Because if I grasp and cling to lesser things, I may never discover what my heart *really* longs for. We are called to make space for Something infinitely greater.

So how does one let go? How do we make space? Augustine calls it *delectatio victrix*: victorious allurement, conquering delight. It is not simply the result of our personal efforts. Discipline has its value, but the real conversion is a work of grace. "Cast yourself upon him," Augustine heard within himself; in trying to "stand on your own strength, you stand not."[5] It is one of the central themes of Augustine's works: that of nature and grace. As we will see later on, Augustine strongly emphasized the role of grace in our lives, as opposed to his contemporaries who claimed that human efforts were central to the spiritual life. He spoke of conversion as an act of receptivity: it is a surrender to God's "drawing attraction," "conquering allurement." This is the work of grace in us.

The idea remains significant today. Often, in various religious circles, sacrifice and discipline are viewed as holy. Now, don't get me wrong: it is true that they are a part of life. Love sometimes requires sacrifice, and achieving any goal requires some discipline. But they are a means to an end. Self-denial, for its own sake, teeters dangerously on pride. (Somehow, that looks more hard-core than relaxing into what is.) Instead of trying to check all the boxes on the "I'm OK" list, the invitation is to listen to the divine beckonings. Where is he alluring you now? Where is the invitation to let go? Where does your death grip on reality cause tension and strife? It may not look as grandiose as we want, but gentle acceptance will bring us much more quickly to the thing we want. Happiness.

For Augustine, the invitation was to let go of his playboy lifestyle. He had begun to taste and see the sweetness of spiritual realities, but found himself unable to untangle himself from his distractions. However, as the *delectatio victrix* began to work in his soul, the desire for heavenly things grew stronger and he slowly was freed from his addiction. "All my empty dreams suddenly lost their charm and my heart began to throb with a bewildering passion for the wisdom of eternal truth...My God, *how I burned with longing* to have wings to carry me back to you, away from all earthly things, although I had no idea what you would do with me!"[6]

This is a sigh of relief for all of us would-be conquerors. *We don't have to spearhead this ourselves!* The *divine* does the heavy lifting. We cannot muscle ourselves into surrender. In my part of the world, the breadbasket of America, this is a particularly difficult concept to grasp. We're hardy folk here. We pull ourselves up by our own bootstraps. We'd lend a hand to anyone who needs it, but of course *we* would never need help ourselves. We've got it all together. Historically, we had to: the winters killed off anyone less than stalwart.

It takes some un-learning for us to be dependent again. It's not that we can't take care of ourselves. We have been given skills and talents for a reason. But that reason is not to put Reality in a headlock and not let go until it conforms to our wishes. We need to remember how to be gentle, like the calloused man who becomes a father for the first time. Imagine holding your newborn infant. Observe your baby's powerlessness, and let your heart soften. Recognize how unprepared you are to control Reality. Ask for the strength to let go, to hold Reality gently. You cannot hold a newborn like you hold a sledgehammer.

For this reason I love the Twelve Step movement. Twelve Step groups have been around for decades, helping people let go of their addictions to alcohol, drugs, food, gambling, sex, people pleasing, and control. (Who *doesn't* have an addiction to one of those things??) The starting point of everything they do is to recognize their powerlessness over their dependencies. They rely on a Higher Power to give them the strength they need to find freedom. It requires immense humility, and an immense dependence on grace. At its base, it means becoming comfortable with your own poverty.

This is the heart of spirituality. All genuine movements of Spirit are trying to bring you closer to a deep acceptance of Reality. Which is easier said than done! It includes not only a welcoming of your present situation, but also of all your own flaws, limitations, desires and dreams. It means accepting others, with all *their* flaws, life decisions, and infuriating habits.

Knowing the difference between what I can control and what I can't control is half the battle. Some things call out to be changed: we can adjust our attitude, stop people pleasing (just say no, for goodness' sake!), or put up healthy boundaries. But think of how many times we try to "fix" our situation or those around us. I cannot control your infuriating behavior, beyond asking you to stop. I can't always convert you to my way of thinking. I cannot avoid the flow of seasons that bring death or life.

This is what it means to die to ourselves. It's a death of our expectations and lesser desires. We might want perfectly reasonable things, but the divine might have other plans. Not because he doesn't want to give us what we need, but because we often don't know what we need.

I have a friend named Amy who is a homeschooling mom. Part bohemian, part minimalist, Amy has more spark (and snark) than a lot of people I know. Over the past decade, Amy has lost several children due to miscarriage. She explained to me how grieving the loss of one of her children led to an even deeper discovery:

> A few years ago I was pregnant with twins. I was thrilled. But after a couple of previous miscarriages, I had a precarious relationship with hope. Could I actually let myself get excited? Could I dream about my little boy and my little girl playing together? Could I believe that God wanted that for me? Unfortunately, I lost one of the twins along the way. The loss of this little girl brought back all the grief from my previous miscarried children, and it hurt. A lot. I wept, grappled, and sometimes numbed out the pain.
>
> Everything changed at book club one night. We were discussing how our desires are always so much deeper than they appear. That, at the root of all our longings, is an ache for the Infinite. This shocked me out of my numbness. With sudden clarity, I realized: it wasn't just my baby I wanted. Yes, I missed little Clara—but the intensity of the ache was not about just my lost child. It was so much bigger than that. She couldn't fill that void—nor could a hundred babies!
>
> This was mind blowing for me! It even reawakened my hope—which was a weird thing to experience in

the middle of all the pain. But realization dawned on me: wait, I'm *supposed* to feel this?? It was as if I had been running around screaming to everyone, 'I have two eyes! I have TWO eyes! TWO!' — feeling like a freak of nature, and freaking myself out because of it. But that night, someone grabbed my face, looked sternly into my TWO eyes, and said, 'Yes, Amy. LOOK,' double pointing to her own pair of eyes. 'WE ALL DO.'

What a relief! I'm normal! I'm not alone! It felt so freeing: 'Yes, Amy, *we all ache.*' And that is what is at the base of everything else we long for.

·

Amy found freedom. In recognizing her dependence on Something Infinite to make her whole, she could look up from her grief and see the horizon for the first time. That's what the divine does for us. He helps us loosen our grip on our smaller desires, so we can open our palms to receive something far greater. Let me repeat: *he* helps us let go. When releasing and accepting seem impossible (you don't need to start a death grip on that, too! —) rely on the divine to carry you.

Our desires serve a good purpose, then. Whether misguided (addictions, control) or benign (authentic friendship, beautiful scenery), they always whisper to us of deeper yearnings. They are echoes of the true joy we're all seeking. But an *echo* implies that there is an original Word that was spoken. It brings us hope.

"Like cold water to a thirsty soul, so is good news from a far country."[7] Familiar echoes are refreshing, like 'cold water;' but they are also tantalizing. We want it *all*. The vastness of the starry night sky was this for our mystic friend John. It was not simply an aesthetic experience, but spoke to John of God, giving him a promise that more was to come. The beauty that so attracted Augustine similarly worked to draw him out of and beyond himself. "I asked the sea and the deeps, and the creeping things that lived, and they replied, 'We are not your God; seek higher than we.'"[8] The danger is in stopping at the things and not letting them carry us beyond.

CS Lewis expresses it masterfully:

The books or the music in which we thought the beauty was located will betray us if we trust to them; it was not in them, it only came through them, and what came through them was longing. These

53

things — the beauty, the memory of our own past — are good images of what we really desire; but if they are mistaken for the thing itself they turn into dumb idols, breaking the hearts of their worshippers. For they are not the thing itself; they are only the scent of a flower we have not found, the echo of a tune we have not heard, news from a country we have never yet visited.[9]

Augustine was a "worshipper" with his heart broken, and only through a slow process of conversion — *delectatio victrix* — was able to start his pilgrim path back to that country he had never yet visited.

What it is: "I know not what"

If the echo is only a hint of a "tune we have not heard," how will we recognize the melody when we do hear it? What name to give to the source of all our desire? "We cannot stop reaching out for it, and yet we know that all we can experience or accomplish is not what we yearn for. This unknown 'thing' is the true hope which drives us, and at the same time the fact that it is unknown is the cause of all forms of despair and also of all efforts."[10]

Here we cross into the realm of the ineffable, where the only path is the *via negativa*. Because it has to do with the infinite, our terminology cannot contain it. I can dance around it, tell you what it's not, or give you analogies. ("God is like the sun, always present but sometimes hidden, giving life to all." "I long for you as I do for running streams, in a dry, weary land without water." "The infinite will be a perfect union of all things.") The problem is, if it's infinite, how could we possibly contain it in words?

Augustine attempts to describe this big Something we want, but is dissatisfied with his results. Sometimes he calls it "eternal life."[11] But the connotations of these words are misleading. "Life" connotes

> We get closer to "knowing" God by loving and desiring him than by speaking or thinking about him.

the life that we have now — and who wants that for all eternity? ("Is that it? Wouldn't I get bored?") He tries other analogies, like gold and honey and wine. "But who will claim that in that one syllable we utter the full expanse of our heart's desire? Whatever we say is necessarily less than the full truth." [12] We cannot capture God. To paraphrase another mystic: if you think you understand God, it is not God you have understood.

John often gives up on language. He calls the object of our desire the "I-know-not-what." He *tasted* that wonderful Something in his mystical experiences, but had fewer and fewer things to say about it. His expressions became more obscure the deeper he went: "I entered into unknowing, and there I remained unknowing, transcending all knowledge."[13] Our human brains can't do it. We get closer to "knowing" God by loving and desiring than by speaking or thinking. In the end, the only adequate response is silence. Words cincture the reality to which they refer; silence, in the very least, allows a reality to roam free. As it is with the most sacred, "the abundant meanings of the Holy Spirit cannot be caught in words."[14]

"Bridegroom"

If silence is the best response, then when we must speak, the saints agree that imagery and symbols are the best means to communicate the incommunicable.[15] John's primary metaphor is that of spousal union. Surprisingly, many mystics find a close kinship between authentic spirituality and authentic sexuality. It makes sense: our sexual longings reflect the inner dynamism of God. He is a communion of persons. Isn't that precisely what sexuality draws us to?

For John, our longing is like the bride longing for consummation with her bridegroom. His whole *Spiritual Canticle* is the song of a lovesick Bride, in search of her Bridegroom. She, the symbol of the soul, is "sick with love,"[16] and cannot stand to have anything but her Beloved. "Give me thyself at once! Send me no more messengers."[17] Anything but the object of her desire — which she still calls the "I know not what" — will not stop her longing. Yet her canticles tell us that union is possible: "In the inner wine cellar/...there He gave me His breast;/ There He taught me a sweet and living knowledge;/ And I gave myself to Him,/ Keeping nothing back;/ There I promised to be His bride."[18] The union reaches its height in his poem *The Living Flame of Love,* which dances around the consummation with exclamations and ejaculatory phrases:

> O sweet cautery,
> O delightful wound!

> O gentle hand! O delicate touch
> That tastes of eternal life…
> How gently and lovingly
> You wake in my heart…
> And by Your sweet breathing,
> Filled with good and glory,
> How tenderly You swell my heart with love!

The consummation is a dark one. Almost all of his poetry mentions a silencing of the senses, a transcending of the knowledge, a giving-up on language. Yet even while ineffable, the gift of the divine Bridegroom is so sublime that it is unmistakable. It is the "I-know-not-what, which is so gladly found."[19]

"Homeland"

While John prefers spousal imagery, Augustine, on the other hand, prefers the image of home. His longing is a nostalgia. We are pilgrims on this earth, and life is a return journey to the home we left behind us. "There is some one thing towards which we must be heading, when we toil amid the manifold engagements of this life. Now we head for this as being yet in pilgrimage, and not in our abiding place; as yet on the way, not yet in our country; as yet in longing, not yet in enjoyment. Yet let us head towards it, and that without sloth and without intermission, that we may some time be able to reach it."[20] We are always "on the way," "passing through," and therefore rightfully groan in our longing.[21] Because we have not yet reached our destination, we cannot rejoice in all the delights of home—but the vision of such things draws us.

In some ways, longing is both the path and the fuel. This is the whole point of all of our prayers and rituals and sacraments: "that this longing may not only be implanted and germinate, but also *expand* to such a measure of capacity as to be fit to take in what eye hath not seen, nor ear heard, nor hath entered into the heart of man."[22] This is the call: stop and stay. When your spiritual practice leads to a quiet yearning, you have found the path. "Remain here, and you will find what you are looking for," it seems to whisper. Remaining can feel uncomfortable, as the longing will likely grow— but it will serve as the inner fuel needed to stay the path.

This pilgrimage of longing is one of the central themes of Augustine's masterpiece, *City of God*. Man is a *peregrinus*, he says (translated pilgrim, wayfarer, or sojourner); he is a citizen of the City of God, sojourning in the City of Man. Reaching our homeland is our life's goal; here below, we only experience a sense of it, an echo. "The glorious city of God is my theme in this work... a city surpassingly glorious, whether we view it as it still lives, sojourning as a stranger... or as it shall dwell in the fixed stability of its eternal seat, which it now waits with patience for... final victory and perfect peace."[23] Life is our Odyssey. We travel, adventure, battle and search; all with the hopes of returning home. Longing helps keep the memory alive and the ship pointed toward home.

For Augustine, it really is a memory. He believed that we were all created by the One source of all Being. He also believed that something in us remembers that experience. In some dark and pre-rational way, we sense where we come from and where we truly belong. It reminds me of the story a friend told me. His daughter, age four, was delighted at the arrival of her baby brother. She would ask to hold him on the couch, and cradle him with all the sisterly love she could muster. One night, my friend found his daughter looking over the crib while the infant slept. "Baby," she whispered, her face earnest and eyes solemn. "Can you tell me what God is like? I'm beginning to forget."

We all begin to forget. Whatever inklings we have of a home with perfect joy, tender love, and a peace where everyone gets along — is dismissed as fantasy. But something that is fantasy in this life may not be fantasy elsewhere. And if we want to get "elsewhere", we may need to begin questioning our scientific reasoning and tune in to the inklings. What do they have to say to us?

"Come home."

Come home to the place you know you belong. This is the place your soul slips away to, when you look longingly into the sunset or recall, with a wistful smile, the laughter of a loved one since passed. The nostalgia means something: They are all here. Waiting for you.

4

Where does it come from?

Once I was on a tour in a small museum in the Midwest. I was a young girl, curious and wide-eyed as ever, taking in all the mysterious artifacts that surrounded me. The tour guide held one up for the group to see. "Take a look at this one. What do you suppose it was for?"

Two dozen pairs of little eyes looked up at the object. Many screwed up and squinty faces tried to make sense of the rusty contraption, complete with cogs, levers, and doodads. "Anyone have any guesses?"

"I bet you could hurt someone with it," said one, looking at his younger brother mischievously.

"Probably could! But we're not going to do that today. Anyone else?"

We remained silent. "It's a corn grinder. Its purpose is to grind corn. See—" he pointed— "the dried corn goes in here, and these wheels grind it, and out here comes corn meal. Settlers used to use it a very long time ago."

The tour guide proceeded to the next exhibit, explaining the difficult life of homesteaders. I walked away that day with an important life lesson.

What could I possibly have learned about life from a corn grinder?

Things make sense when you know what they're for.

The levers and cogs made sense once I knew the purpose of the contraption. "Oh! It grinds corn! And the meal comes out here. I get it." Screwed up faces relax and raise into looks of understanding and interest. We nod at each other. "Of course. I don't know how I didn't see that."

How much easier would life be if we had that same facial transformation regarding our own selves?

That is, what does it mean to be human?

•

If our inner inklings are any indication, we are made for something vast. Most spiritual traditions would refer to it as a sort of union. We try our best to speak to it with what language we have: a coming home to oneself, a mystical, spousal union with God, a becoming one with the One.

If this is the purpose of our lives, then longing, as some traditions would say, is programmed into our DNA so that we would have a roadmap home. The lack we feel is actually a capacity. Its dimensions hint at Who we are meant to receive there. We all experience the ache of that space in different ways, drawing us to write and compose and seek adventure and make love. At the root is always this tension we are trying to work out in ourselves.

These are the "cogs and levers" that make up our own humanity. Behavior — our own and others' — begins to make a lot more sense when we recognize what is driving it. Even when we are unconscious of it, we are responding to the beckoning of a Lover.

The clincher is that our Lover is also our archetype.

Origins in the Divine

Our spiritual DNA is modeled after Someone. While we may not be exact replicas, we are somehow mysteriously tangled up with the divine. We exist. We love. We create. We move and live within his energy-breath-spirit (pick your term). And our deepest longings are a participation in his longings.

You see, Infinite Love cannot be "love" if it does not include desire. This is plain on a very natural level. What spouse wants to be in a relationship in which they do not feel desired? Lacking that, the warmth and familiarity become replaced by duty, or perhaps a loyalty from which all fire has been extinguished. Desire implies a deep acceptance, and an affirmation of the good of the other. "I love you so much that I want to be with you, to be united to you. I desire you."

In this way, desire is one of the greatest gifts we can give to another. It is the gift of receptivity. Being received by someone in love, whether in a physical or spiritual way, is one of the most life-affirming experiences we can have. When a wife opens herself to receive her husband in sexual intimacy, or when a trusted friend allows you to share your deepest hurts or hopes with them, you feel seen. These are healing, expansive encounters. And they mirror the inner life of the divine.

For John and Augustine, God is a trinity: he is Lover, Beloved, and the Love between them. Each Person longs for the Other, and receives the Other's gift of self. It is a generous outpouring between Lovers. Long-

> We are so intertwined with the divine we do not realize he is our very breath. We breathe in Existence; Being; Love; we exhale, with everything else, the life and energy and connectedness of all that exists.

ing with an infinite cavity; pouring Oneself out for sheer goodness; receiving Other as gift and delight. It becomes an ebb and flow of the erotic (*eros*= desirous love) and the agapic (*agape*= self-giving love).

John writes ballads of this cosmic exchange. He sees the Son as having infinite caverns, begging to be filled. The Father delightfully whispers,

"Nothing, my Son, pleases me,
but your company.
"If something is sweet,
through you alone do I taste it.
The more of you I see in its reflection,

the wider my smile;

"What is unlike you,
has nothing of me.
In you alone is my delight,
life of my life!
"You are the fire of my fire,
my knowing;
the form of my substance,
in you am I well pleased.

"Whoever gives his love to you, my Son,
to him I give myself,
and him I fill
with the love I feel for you
just for making you beloved,
my Beloved."[24]

John sees the divine as pure generosity and de-light. Because of his overabundance, he desires to share it. It is the nature of goodness to share itself, to make it more abundant—so God creates. He creates galaxies and dark matter and supernova; bubbling brooks and mitochondria and praying mantises. He creates humans modeled after his own nature, wrought with this beautifully frustrating tension that draws us out of ourselves into union. One can almost feel the mirth of God: with a sparkle in his eye, he wants all of us to be drawn and then fulfilled, as he is.

John's vision:

"My Son, I wish to give you
a bride who will love you...
that she may know the good
I have in such a Son;
and rejoice with me
in your grace and fullness."

"I am very grateful,"
the Son answered;
"I will show my brightness
to the bride you give me,
so that by it she may see
how great my Father is,
and how I have received
my being from your being.
I will hold her in my arms
and she will burn with your love,
and with eternal delight
she will exalt your goodness."
"Let it be done, then," said the Father,
for your love has deserved it.[25]

Who is the Bride? She is you and me. *We* are the gift, created by the Father and given to the Son. We are the one held in the Son's arms so that we might "burn with love, and eternal delight." We are welcomed into Love's embrace! This remarkable claim is already a reality. We are so intertwined with the divine we do not realize he is our very breath. We breathe in Existence; Being; Love; we exhale, with everything else, the life and energy and connectedness of all that exists.

Take a moment to let that soak in.

Notice your breathing, your oneness with the divine.

He created us to experience *delight*. Not just contentment, or OK-ness. Delight is laughter, bliss, effusiveness. We breathe it in; are tangled up with it. So, too, are the tree branches waving outside your window, the stardust across galaxies, and the currents of the sea. We are all invited to participate in the cosmic play. Our distinction is that we can consciously choose participation: we can relax into the fun, or we can resist and boycott.

The choice is ours. We can allow our desires to draw us into the eternal love story, or we can pout. But when we see the bigger picture — when we recognize *we are desired*, and that our own sense of longing is an invitation to join the play — why would anyone choose to pout?

PART II: PRAYER AND DESIRE

5

Can our Desire be Fulfilled?

In high school I took an independent study class. We had the entire quarter to pick a theme, read a handful of books on the topic, and produce a few projects that demonstrated we had learned something. The class was loosely structured and allowed me to explore whatever I was most curious about at the time. I chose the broad topic of religion and spirituality.

What I remember most from the course was not the books I read, but a conversation I had with a fellow student one day. He was sitting in the hall outside the classroom (apparently to read), and I decided to follow suit. We began to discuss our chosen topics, and I asked him if he believed in God. "No, not really," he drawled. I paused, trying to make sense of this in my head." So... if you don't believe in God, what do you live for?" The question was an earnest one.

"Nothing, I guess."

I started a little. "Wow. Sounds kind of depressing." I realized after the words were out that they weren't my most tactful. But it was an honest response, and I didn't know how to say it any more gracefully.

"Yeah. That's why I do pot."

The words sunk in like an anvil in a lake. They made perfect, complete sense to me. If life was meaningless, why not do whatever yielded the least amount of pain?

•

The difference between hope and hopelessness is found in the answer to the question: can our desire be fulfilled? Is there meaning to what happens to me and my desires? And if there is meaning and a chance of fulfillment, is it possible in this lifetime?

If fulfillment were impossible, we would be condemned to a senseless life. Yearning would have no satisfaction. Desire would only call for a numbing agent and flat living. One day would follow the next without direction. The restlessness would be meaningless.

If, on the other hand, fulfillment is possible, hope is the sweet but painful promise that we will return home. It would mean that longings are beckonings. And that the One who beckons is waiting for us on the threshold.

Prayer: longing and fulfillment

John and Augustine have their own way of responding to the question of hope. Is fulfillment possible? Yes and no, Augustine and John respond—and both the *yes* and the *no* are what they define as prayer. Far from our reductionist concepts of devotions and mindless petitions, our mystics call the whole ambit of longing – darkness – I-don't-know-what – echoes – consummation – "*prayer.*" "The entire life of a good Christian is in fact an exercise of holy desire."[26] "There is your prayer, in your longing."[27] "In order to obtain this true blessed life, he who is himself the true blessed Life has taught us to pray… with desire, by which we may receive what he prepares to bestow."[28] Desire prepares us for the *bestowal*, which is the culmination of prayer.

Yet, too, the longing already is the prayer. Far be it from us to say that only the culmination of divine union is worthy of the name 'prayer.' The whole process of wooing and desiring and finally union of selves is 'prayer'; the same goes for the union between two spouses. True, the consummation gives meaning and value to the romancing that precedes it; yet it would be simplistic to call only the climax an expression of love.

In fact, prayer as desire is what allows us to follow the call to "pray always."[29] Obviously we cannot be on our knees twenty-four hours a day, nor can our minds constantly be engaged with spiritual things when daily life must continue. (I cannot be actively meditating while organizing a work project or talking to my mother.) But longing — longing is something that can continue, as an accompaniment to all that we do. "There is another prayer, interior and uninterrupted: our longing," says Augustine.[30] This type of prayer requires neither the structure of time nor the structure of words. When words *are* used, it is to "excite ourselves" to desire more.[31] It is precisely to this desire that all of our other devotions and meditations should tend: in fact, when the soul reaches such a state of "attention," Augustine advises us to stop and stay. Sense a beckoning? Look up from your book; disregard the beads for a moment. Be with Being. Soak in the moment of stillness. If it is given, let your "heart throb with continuous pious emotion toward" God. For in some cases, "prayer consists more in groaning than in speaking, in tears rather than in words."[32]

> Our mystics call the whole ambit of longing – darkness – I-don't-know-what – echoes – consummation – "prayer."

A friend once used the image of surfing to explain prayer. Like prayer, surfing requires a lot of waiting. You paddle out on your board, and then you wait for the swells. It can be a very peaceful, spiritual experience. Soaking in the warm Pacific water. Moving with the rhythm of the swells. Using all your senses to feel when the next wave is coming. When the gift comes, you paddle, hop on your board, and use your muscle memory to balance and ride that wave wherever it takes you. This may be a very brief experience, or, on occasion, you land a long, perfect barrel in which you somehow become one with the water. You don't decide when the waves come: you simply show up, *be*, and receive the gifts that the Ocean has for you that day.

The quality of the experience is not up to us. I may or may not have Augustine's intense emotions. I may feel achey and melancholy; but I may also feel flatness or stillness, joy or triumph. What's important is not so much the tool (the surfboard) or the emotion (it matters little to the Ocean), but more so the posture of receptivity. One can understand why surfing is such a spiritual experience for so many people. Like prayer, it requires simple attentiveness to the vast Ocean, and openness to its gifts.

John sees prayer similarly. To him, it is a loving attention, a receptivity: this is what it means to be poor in spirit. To have space to receive the Other. Method matters little. Place, posture, book, beads, in assembly, alone: the one requisite thing is that we surrender and give Love entrance. He is already present within; inviting, desiring. All we need to do is enter within ourselves and "desire him there, adore him there."[33] We need not seek anything else. "What more do you want, O soul! And what else do you search for outside, when within yourself you possess your riches, delights, satisfactions, fullness, and kingdom—your Beloved whom you desire and seek? Be joyful and gladdened in your interior recollection with him, for you have him so close to you."[34]

The gift is ready to be given. Are we ready to receive it? Our part in prayer is to show up and make space, "exciting" or expanding our desire inasmuch as possible. If the sweetness of honey is ready to be poured—in fact, is hovering, poised mid-air over the container—we need to let go of what "sour wine" remains. First we must show up.

Our part: return to the Interior

John and Augustine agree that the place of encounter with the divine is within, in our heart's deepest core. John calls it the "inner wine cellar," the soul's "deepest center" where the divine wounds us and unites himself to us.[35] He goes so far as to say that God *is* the center of our soul—not only that he is located there.[36] Or, as Augustine put it, the Spirit is "more intimate to us than we are to ourselves."[37] Interestingly, for Christian mystics, the transcendent is found within us. The things on the outside serve to bring us in. "I replied unto all the things which encompass the door of my flesh: 'You have told me of my God, that you are not he; tell me something of him.' And they cried out with a loud voice, 'He made us.' ...These things did my inner man know by the ministry of the outer."[38]

Searching outside ourselves is fruitless, if him whom we want is within. "Why do we go forth and run to the heights of the heavens and the lowest parts of the earth, seeking him who is within us, if we wish to be with him?"[39] Augustine had done plenty of this "running" in his own life, searching in vain for rest for his soul. While recognizing the beauty and goodness of the earth, he knew these things could distract him if they did not conduct him back to his center. "I searched for you outside myself, while all along you were within me. You were in me, but I was not in You."[40]

Augustine's experience is not foreign to our own. Frequently we seek "more" of whatever we think brings fulfillment, only to recognize—perhaps after years of searching—that what we really want can be found within. The journey is an interior one. The path is simple, if not always intuitive: by the way of self-knowledge we reach divine knowledge; by descending into our own depths, we reach transcendent heights. "Enter, then, into your heart and if you have faith, you will find Christ there. There Christ speaks to you."[41]

How do we enter into our heart? As usual, it is a combination of human willingness and divine grace. We must 'show up,' and 'make room,' but *even this willingness is a gift to us,* like the "light" which led Augustine. "Being admonished by all of this to return to myself, O Lord, I entered my own depths with you as my guide, and I was able to do it because you were my helper."[42] The divine helps us relax into ourselves and release all of the distractions that flutter before our eyes. To-do lists, judgments, and inner critics must not be so much overcome as noticed and released. I don't have to mentally wrestle these out of my sphere of attention. Instead, they can become part of the experience.

Part of the 'making space' also involves clearing out the noise and clutter within. It is only after we release our grasp on our daily distractions that we can arrive at God.[43] The noise and distractions may even be of the good kind. Things like music, technology, spiritual reading or devotions have nothing inherently wrong with them. Some of these can even help us transition into the silence. However, as with other structures and methods, even good "noise" must be allowed to fade away so we can leave space for the Word to come. Says Augustine:

If the tumult of the body were silenced — silenced the phantasies of earth, waters, and air — silenced, too, the heavens; yea, the very soul be silenced to herself, and go beyond herself by not thinking of herself — silenced all dreams and revelations, every tongue, and every sign... having roused only our ears to him who created them, and he alone speak... that we may hear his word... If this could be sustained, and other visions of a far different kind be withdrawn, and this one ravish, and absorb, and envelope its beholder amid these inward joys, so that his life might be eternally like that one moment of knowledge which we now sighed after — is not this 'Enter into the joy of Your Lord'?[44]

Silence requires a certain letting go, which is not always easy. Once the clamor begins to fade we are left to face ourselves, and we do not always like what we see. There are certain things we prefer to keep buried, well-hidden under feet of defenses, blindness, and plastered smiles. Yet the more we unearth, the more room the divine has to fill. It is this inner space of silence that we must foster. Having done so, Augustine and John assure us of encounter: not because it is something we have procured or can bring about, but because God is already there, waiting for us to give him permission to fill our cavities and fulfill our longings.[45]

God's part: grace, gift

Our task, then, is always tied to God's initiative. Our job is to receive. The filling and fulfilling is always a gratuitous gift. We can only prepare ourselves by becoming receptive to the God who is longing to give; but *when* and *how* he gives is up to him. We wait, we meditate, "like a dry, weary land without water;"[46] when the Spirit decides to give the rain, we call it contemplation. Here John calls us to leave behind our methods and meditations and "be with" the divine. "Regarding... vocal prayer and other devotions, one should not become attached to any ceremonies or modes of prayer other than those Christ taught us."[47] "Since you know that in your heart your Beloved, for whom you long, dwells hidden, your concern must be to *be with him* in hiding, and there in your heart you will embrace him."[48]

When the Spirit comes to dwell, form matters little. Form serves more as a launching pad, which may be returned to as needed, but never clung to if we ever have the hopes of flying. Augustine, too, cautions against formalism: "Far be it from us either to use 'much speaking' in prayer, or to refrain from prolonged prayer, if fervent attention of the soul continue."[49] The whole point is to make space for union — so what would it serve if the infinite God began to pour but we kept fussing with our containers?

The final purpose of the capacity is *gift*. This translates not-our-efforts. If we boast of having achieved something ourselves, what we have grasped is "something other than God."[50] Augustine spent much of his life arguing this. Some of his contemporaries, the Pelagians, thought growth and holiness were achieved through our own efforts. Enough discipline, penance, and practices, and you can arrive at heaven's door! (Or today: If I just follow my checklist — fifteen minutes of meditation a day, go to church on Sunday, and donate to charities — I'm OK!) Augustine, by contrast, was convinced that all was grace. Our efforts have little to do with it, for the goal of life (and therefore prayer) is *union*, not an earnable-perfection. If it were any other way, only the best and brightest could be capable of prayer or fulfillment. Fortunate for us, our very makeup renders us capable of communion. We just need to learn to get out of the way.

This is where John's theme of the *nada* enters in. Unfortunately, this 'buzz word' of John's *Dark Night* is often seen in a bleak light: *nada* does not exactly have the most uplifting of connotations. We think of dryness, abandoning hope, confusion, emptiness. But John speaks of the *nada* much more positively: we must make space, enter into the *nada* in order to make room for the *todo*, which is already hovering, pressing in. Here again is the priority of grace. "Progress will be measured, less by ground covered, more by the amount of room God is given to maneuver," says author Iain Matthews.[51] And God gives "wherever there is room—always showing himself gladly along the highways and byways."[52]

Given this, one can understand why the preferred image of John and most of the mystics is spousal. Our 'restless' God woos us, drawing us to himself by placing his own longing within us. All he wants is to give and to receive our gift. He "allures" (*delectatio*) us and prepares us for his gift of self through the infinite desire he carved within us.[53] It is our cavity, our capacity, and our great dignity. Thus it is only logical that if we are called to such great heights, we will suffer the ache of such great capacities.[54]

John refers to this dignity with the term "bride." We are made for communion. Receptivity ('space,' *'nada'*) is our watchword; John asks us to wait, "not striving, in nakedness and emptiness"[55] for the Bridegroom to come. This is far from comfortable. Stripping ourselves of our self-constructed defenses leaves us vulnerable, and we are not always so sure that union is coming. It may be something initiated externally: a lost job, lost esteem, lost friendship. Something on which we (falsely) constructed our identity is taken away from us, so that our true selves might be given freedom and enabled for communion. The questions that begin to emerge are frightening—perhaps I was wrong to trust? Who am I, if not who they say I am? On what do I depend for my sense of stability? If she can fall, is anyone good? Is anything true?—yet when engaged, these reveal new depths and a surer foundation. We begin to realize how many constructs and makeshift scaffolding we have been using to hold ourselves up. When these fall away, we have no other choice but to depend on the divine to sustain us.

The same goes for the spiritual life. Consolations, feelings of the presence of God, and fruitful meditations are all good, so long as they just as quickly fall away as soon as they lead us to God himself. We want the Bridegroom, not just his gifts.

When we no longer find the divine in our usual ways, it can feel completely disorienting. Or more: it can feel like we're regressing. I've seen it in my own life. When God would move deeper, I'd question what I was doing wrong, instead of considering that it may have been God who moved. If we're used to relaxing together in the living room, and our Lover has moved to the bedroom, we don't need to have a little freak out that he left us. If you're quiet enough, you may realize this is an invitation.

For this reason, the mystics tell us, *nada* is not to be feared. Nakedness is where intimacy happens. As Augustine put it, longing, that visceral, dare-I-hope desire, is "the womb of the heart."[56] That is where we are 'capable' of conceiving the divine Word.

So we conclude that fulfillment is *possible* — but why doesn't he come? Why do we all wander around this watery earth as walking *thirsts*? Even those of us who have embarked on the interior journey don't feel entirely satisfied. If I have journeyed within, encountered my own longing and 'capacity,' and discovered that there was already a Presence within, waiting for me — where is the disconnect? If interiority is the "sure place of encounter," why must I still suffer the pain of restlessness?

There are two answers that John and Augustine give us, and they have to do with waiting. Waiting in "nakedness" is indeed painful, but it stretches our capacity for an even greater gift that is coming. Yet the pain of the first is nothing compared to the intensity of the second: it is John's "wound," the already-but-not-yet, in which we are not left in our nakedness but experience a real taste of divine union. Yet a taste is only partial, and once our appetites have been whet, the sweet and agonizing desire for fullness will never let us rest.

6

Why the Pain?

Not everyone walks around moaning because of their existential ache. (Fortunately.) However, in tracing the path of my own prayer and sharing with dozens of other "seekers", I realized that the experience of longing is a common one. Finding it in the writings of mystics and poets and philosophers and artists confirmed the fact that many of us feel this acutely. One friend of mine described her experience with simplicity.

"Sunsets are my time with God. All my kids know that that is mom's special time, and will often point out to me a sunset that I was too distracted to notice. They gasp: 'Mom! A sunset!' With eyes aglow, they croon, 'It's beautiful...'

"I love to walk to the edge of my subdivision to where fields begin and sky takes over the landscape. It's so beautiful it hurts. Somehow I want to be there, in it. Inside of it. I know it's like wanting to reach the end of a rainbow, expecting a pot of gold, but I can't help it. Somehow I know this is more real, and that God is in it, speaking to me."

What is he saying, I ask?

She pauses, eyes glistening. "It's a promise. Someday I'll be home."

•

Nearly all of us can recall the pain of homesickness. While we may long for a physical home, perhaps even more poignant is the homesickness for a person: someone we lost who felt like home. Someone who was a part of our landscape, our support structure, and our daily interactions. Their absence causes us to ache for them terribly. We long for what we presently cannot have.

While memories and whispers on the wind may eventually bring a wistful comfort, these are nothing close to the reality. In the spiritual realm, the same is true.

Stretching

Our capacity is our poverty. In encountering our restlessness, we realize that we are dependent on something outside of us. Every other need I uncover within me points to that one aching need in my deepest core. My striving for attention or needing to prove my worth are only symptomatic of my need for God. Yet as we said, our poverty is also our dignity, our deepest wealth. It makes us capable of receiving the infinite God.

However, in the end we are finite creatures. How will it ever be possible to fit an infinite God within us? This is one of the causes of our pain. We long for the infinite but can't seem to fit it within the confines of our person, as deep as our caverns are. And though it will never be possible to contain the infinite — this would be contrary to its own definition — we can infinitely grow our caverns to continually fit more and more.[57] "Longing makes the heart grow deep," says Augustine.[58]

Our bishop of Hippo uses the example of stretching a wineskin. Our capacity is too small to receive the greatness of the gift that is coming, so the Spirit goes about enlarging us:

Suppose you are going to fill some holder or container, and you know you will be given a large amount. Then you set about stretching your sack or wineskin or whatever it is. Why? Because you know the quantity you will have to put in it and your eyes tell you there is not enough room. By stretching it, therefore, you increase the capacity of the sack, and this is how God deals with us. Simply by making us wait he increases our desire, which in turn enlarges the capacity of our soul, making it able to receive what is to be given to us.[59]

The function of waiting, then, is to make us "able to receive what he is preparing to give us. His gift is very great indeed, but our capacity is too small and limited to receive it."[60] Waiting causes our desires to grow, which causes our pain to grow, but for the sake of an even greater gift.

It can be likened to the fasting that occurs before a large feast. Our hunger deepens, especially with snack food in sight. ("It would be so easy. Just a few bites.") Yet we know that pre-packaged finger food is not what we really want. If we can practice restraint and not immediately gratify our cravings, we will enjoy even more fully the wedding feast that awaits us. The problem is usually that our desires are too small, in regards to what the divine wants to give. We are used to limiting our desires to stave off disappointment. Instead of audaciously asking for a nine-course meal, we ask for a peanut butter sandwich. "I don't want to impose," we think. "The world doesn't work like that anyway." Or – "Why would God give *me* a miracle?"

Do we believe there is a scarcity of grace? That perhaps God has a limited bank account, and surely we are not the most deserving of his dolings – ? Yet John and Augustine dare us to audacity. They – and most every spiritual tradition – challenge us to see the world of abundance around us. Reality is on our side. The divine is infinitely good. Without end. Free flowing love, grace, goodness. If that is the world we live in, why would we cramp our expectations? *Dream big.* Ask big. Open yourself up to the infinite. The secret is that God inspired the root of those desires in the first place.

John invites us: "So the soul must desire with all her desire to come to what in this life lies beyond her mind or the capacity of her heart."[61] What would you ask for if you weren't afraid? If you ignored your inner critic? ("That's just selfish." "That would never happen.") As author Iain Matthew put it, spiritual

growth means "making his generosity, not our poverty, the measure of our expectations."[62]

John traces out the journey of this growth in his
poetry. One might say that the whole *Dark Night* is an
elaboration on the stretching that happens in the waiting. As he described it to his friend Sister Leonor, who
was undergoing the pains of transition from one con-
vent to another, the divine brings us through suffering
because he has a gift to give us:

> It is His Majesty who has done this, to bring you
> greater profit. *For the more he wants to give, the more
> he makes us desire,* till he leaves us empty so as to fill
> us with blessings… God's immense blessings can
> only fit into a heart that is empty. They come in that
> kind of solitude. For this reason, because the Lord
> would love to see you, since he loves you well, well
> and truly alone, intent on being himself all your
> company.[63]

"The more he wants to give, the more he makes
us desire." Of course it's going to ache if he's got an
infinity's worth of glory to give us! To make space for
it all, he stretches us. He plucks out our hoarder's
stash — all that stuff we've been clinging to. And like a
hoarder, we have a conniption that he's throwing away
very important things. "NO! Not that! Not my sense of

control! I was saving that! That was the only thing that made me feel put together!!" "NOT THE WINE! HEY! I NEEDED THAT! HOW AM I SUPPOSED TO-COPE??"

He wants to be "himself all your company." But generally, we don't see that. We see what he's taking away, or asking us to give up. We don't see what's coming. "It is like a traveler going to new lands of which he has no personal knowledge... it will be a journey of uncertainty." [64]The darkness feels bewildering. So we cling to the old, remaining curled up in the fetal position, unable or unwilling to open ourselves to the new.

The key is to loosen our grip enough to consider another option. If our Lover isn't in the living room, is there a chance that he hasn't abandoned us, and is actually in the bedroom?

Darkness is the invitation. It does not represent the withdrawal of God, but his drawing closer. It marks the beginning of rapid spiritual progress, not regress: it is the Spirit taking over.

The challenge is to trust that the divine is moving in ways we do not understand. (I don't know about you, but I don't have an omniscient view of what's happening in the universe. Yet sometimes... I act like I do.) When you're being stretched, try to hear the invitation within. John reminds us that this is a crucial point. If we turn back now, we lose all. We're halfway

> If that is the world we live in,
> why would we cramp our
> expectations? Dream big. Ask big.
> Open yourself up to the infinite.
> The secret is that God inspired the
> root of those desires in the first place.

through Mordor: surely there is something on the other side that can give us enough reason to persevere?

Some "do not have the patience to wait till God gives them what they seek when he so desires...[65] The new terrain is stark and barren, so we want to run or move or squirm or be anywhere but *here*. If we feel anything, it is usually our own messiness. Yet if we succeed in not running from the emptiness, it will reveal to us a deeper communion. Pain has that funny way of unlocking us at the point we cannot unlock ourselves.[66]

I get it. This is not an easy place to be. It feels like we're stuck in the in-between places. It's a weird, hazy landscape, and the path has all but disappeared. Some days, it may feel flat and lifeless. Other days, it might feel terrifying. We gasp, flail, press in. But even without a clear path, progress is being made. This is our introduction to off-roading. And it's bringing us closer to the union we desire.

A word of advice: be exceedingly gentle with yourself during this time. Many of us have never off-roaded before, and we're using spiritual muscles we've never used. Find a companion on the journey. Take breaks to catch your breath and appreciate the view. Scream at the heavens if you need to. Quiet the Critic in your head that shames you for not being "further ahead." It can be a grueling journey, and self-care is needed if you want to prevent "spiritual strain." The Spirit guides us with the breeze—but we won't notice it if we are hellbent on finding the path again.

As John puts it: "To come to what you know not, you must go by a way you know not."[67]

•

The wandering and waiting have an important purpose. John tells us the haze is for our safety: if we could see, we'd assume we knew the way and go run-

ning ahead. What's better: it's part of the divine romance. Darkness and nakedness might seem terrifying, but they can be the context for intimacy if we'd
only relax and realize that our Bridegroom is there
with us. He's trying to romance us and prepare us for
himself, but we're too busy being afraid of the dark.

As he draws us closer to union, our desires become more painful and intense. It's a spiritual foreplay.
John tells us, "When [our] caverns are empty and pure,
the hunger and sense of spiritual longing is more than
can be borne. ...[D]uring this time of the espousal and
expectation... the anxieties of the caverns of the soul
are usually extreme and delicate."[68] In other places he
calls these desires "disintegration" and "infinite
death"[69] as the soul is stretched to its maximum (we're
trying to fit infinity in here). But the throes of death can
be transformed into sublime hope if we choose to trust
that our Lover is with us. For he is not only present,
but he is beckoning, pressing in. In this way, our painful caverns actually serve as points of entry for the divine. The stretching of them are simply the "proximate
preparation" for his gift.

So in a way, the pain of stretching reveals the
greatness of the gift.[70] God not only gives himself, but
also makes us capable of receiving him. He "provokes"

and "invites" us until we are "wide enough, open enough, and capable of himself."[71] Only then shall we be ready for the gift that is coming.

Already-but-not-yet

One kind of suffering accompanies the delay we endure in waiting for the fulfillment of our desire. Another kind comes from having tasted that fulfillment — perhaps only an 'echo' — and then from pining for the desire to have it *all*.

Is there an 'already' in our already-but-not-yet? Have we ever tasted fulfillment?

Both Augustine and John reply affirmatively. If we had not somehow experienced it, how would we know to want it?[72] We have a certain "learned ignorance" from the Spirit, says Augustine, for we "know not what we should pray for as we ought."[73] Yet the Spirit inspires us with "longings" for that great unknown "blessing." Some taste we have had — as has had Augustine — whetting our appetites and causing an indescribable suffering. "I tasted you, and now I hunger and thirst for you. You touched me, and I am inflamed with love of your peace."[74]

Not only do we taste fulfillment in small bites throughout our lifetime. According to Augustine, we once experienced it in its fullness. Hearkening back to the notions of nostalgia and memory, Augustine believed that if we are homesick, it implies that we were once home. Our creation is in the Oneness of Being, and these origins emerge in traces and echoes throughout life, calling us to return. We have been there once, and in some partial way can be there now. ("The kingdom of heaven is within you."[75])

The "already but not yet" is played out in the partiality of it all. Though we are citizens of eternity, we sojourn here below in the City of Man. The two realities are mixed. Until we reach the fullness in heaven, our happiness and fulfillment will come up short. It "is rather the solace of our misery than the positive enjoyment of felicity."[76] He speaks of it knowing that we are missing something; we are still aliens. However, the "already" is also "joy" and "holy inebriation." [77] Though he may downplay the delight by calling it mere "solace" at times (he was a passionate melancholic, after all), at other times he calls it "a breath of serenity and eternity."[78] Any encounter with the divine carries the scent of our homeland.

John also speaks of the incredible pain and delight that this "limited" happiness causes. It is precisely the tasting followed by a longing for more — the already-but-not-yet — that causes our profound discomfort but simultaneous joy. John calls these experiences "spiritual wounds of love." [79] In the opening stanza of the *Spiritual Canticle*, the bride (the soul) laments the absence of her Bridegroom: "Where have You hidden,/ Beloved, and left me moaning?/ You fled like the stag/ After wounding me..."[80] As John explicates his poetry, he reveals that the normal desire of the soul for God — the waiting, the stretching — here is exacerbated by the wound of love. "Especially after the taste of some sweet and delightful communication of the Bridegroom, [the soul] suffers His absence and is left alone and dry... accompanied by a kind of immense torment and yearning to see God."[81] He assures us that this is very "delightful" and "desirable"[82] — it is a true, profound happiness — but because it is not yet the fullness of union, the soul suffers even more terribly than before.

The bride begs for death as the only means of healing. She knows that the presence of the Bridegroom is so intense that the union she longs for means a certain death. As she lies wounded, she "dies because [she does] not die."[83] It is the complaint of a job half-done, the taste of consummation that is all too brief. "Her complaint is not that He wounded her—for the more a loving soul is wounded the more its love is re-paid—but that in sorely wounding her heart, He did not heal her by slaying her completely. The wounds of love are so sweet and delightful that if they do not cause death they cannot satisfy."[84] Infinite union, or "death," alone will suffice.

In order to explain to his readers the urgency and pain of the soul's longing for union, John employs a number of images. The soul is "weary in proportion to its loss," which is infinite, causing it to feel like an "empty vessel waiting to be filled, or like a hungry man craving food, or like a sick person moaning for health, or like one suspended in the air with nothing to lean on."[85] Each of these is consonant with the dynamic of desire and fulfillment: there is a space to be filled, and its non-filling is bewildering. So much so that it seems as if we were suspended mid-air, not in the I'm-floating-on-the-clouds sense, but as if you suddenly backed up off a cliff. Your heart jumps into your throat and you gasp—and now that gasp is extended indefinitely. The urgency is real.

So "why do You fail to fill, satisfy, accompany, and heal?"[86] Where has our divine Lover gone, failing to "slay" the soul so as to bring the union it longs for? Again, John's answer is always found in the context of and call to union. The pain and longing of hope are *already* an experience of God. They are part of the divine romance. John's understanding of Christ made sense of this: his God was crucified. He could relate to our pain, and we to his. "Progress lies only in imitating Christ," says John, and Christ was "annihilated in soul, without any consolation or relief."[87] *He has infinite caverns, too,* John reminds us; it is in his image, after all, that we are created. The cross is where Christ was stripped of all, and stretched to the extreme of his divine identity. For the Christian mystic, it was by such "annihilation" that Christ accomplished his greatest work: he restored to us the possibility of union. His night gave meaning to our night.

Just as in Christ's case, the feeling of being entirely unhinged and abandoned does not mean that we are really so. Though the night disorients us at our deepest core ("My God, my God, why have You abandoned me?"[88]), there is a place still deeper that is somehow *presence*. Even when crucified and feeling abandoned, Jesus was still in union with his Father by the

103

very nature of his *being*—just as God remains in our deepest selves even when all seems lost. The monk pleads with us not to misinterpret this. Uncomfortable, disorienting, bewildering, yes—but also the point of most intimate union. Our wounds become our allies, and prayer becomes the welcoming of the already-present Spirit into those points of access. Union, then, is "measured by one's annihilation for God… not [by] good times and spiritual feelings, but in the living, sensory and spiritual, exterior and interior death of the cross."[89] That, says John, is why we suffer the pain.

7

Our Destiny: Restless Rest

Sometimes I feel like I'm running around with a hole in the bottom of my cup. You know, Oliver-Twist style— wide-eyed, grubby-faced— "Please, sir, I'd like some more!" Frantically, I offer it to anyone I can think of, begging them to fill me. Netflix: "Will you fill my cup?" Friends: "Will you fill my cup?" Black-hole web-browsing: "Will you fill my cup?" Though they may pour me a swig, it doesn't last long before I'm dry again. Stupid hole. The water I do receive is both tantalizing and frustrating.

However, when I take a step back, I wonder: what if I've understood the model all wrong? What if what I'm holding is not a "cup," so to speak, but a con-duit? What if I'm not meant to be filled in a once-and-done kind of way?

If Goodness exists, there is hope for us wander-ers. If there is Love; if Mercy is the world's foundation;

if Being undergirds our being; then there is an infinite Source that mirrors our infinite thirst. If we have a massive "hole" (desire, capacity) within, it is because we were designed that way. Love — Mercy — Being — is pouring himself out, and we were created to continually receive more and more and more and *more*. In order to make space for it, we were made bottomless. Instead of a cup, we're a conduit.

A hole is exactly what you want when you are stationed under a laughing, roaring waterfall.

Mutual indwelling

In this lifetime, our task is to offer as little resistance as possible to the waterfall of grace. As we stretch our capacities and allow our longings to grow, the Spirit pours himself continually into that space. The Christian mystics call it "mutual indwelling," or the "spiritual marriage." It may sound lofty, but there is nothing more *real*. It is becoming one with the One. You are "wrapped up," participating deeply in the divine dynamic of poverty-and-bestowal, longing-and-quenching. Nothing could make you feel more alive, free, or *yourself*.

Beautiful promises, you might think. But what does this look like in the day-to-day? Is it really attainable?

In the everyday, it looks very much like you and me! Mystics still experience pain, have bad moods, and pass gas. Again — there is no fairy dust! They are deeply human, and part of their "advanced state" is that they've learned that they're always learning. They stand before Reality with open palms. They receive whatever comes.

I like to think of us all as buoys, anchored in the deep. We're all designed the same, with a depth that holds us steady, and a flotation device that interfaces with the exterior world. On the surface, movement depends on the weather. Towering waves and violent storms come and thrash our buoys. What does not depend on the weather is our anchor, snuggled firmly and resolutely in the sand far beneath the waves. In the deep, it is dark and still. All you feel are the strong and gentle movements of the currents.

On the surface, we all "bob" the same: both a mystic and an ordinary joe will teeter when a loved one is killed in a car crash, and will totter when deprived of sleep. (Ask anyone who's lived with me: I'm a bear when sick or tired!) What makes the difference is our interior response. When we have a spaciousness within, we have more room to accept whatever Reality chooses to give us. While one buoy reels and says "This is the end! We are all doomed! I am drowning!", another buoy reels and says "I feel incredibly uncomfortable! I have lost my job: what could this possibly mean?" One interprets events and feelings (reeling, losing a job) as a threat; the other holds an open space, without having to assign it a label as good or bad. Same events; very different responses.

When we realize we are so deeply anchored, we innately know that what happens on the surface is not all there is. We are one with the unmovable Earth. We can sense his gentle shifting. The tides tug us, and we respond with suppleness.

If you have ever met a person like this, you remember it clearly. Their serenity is striking. You are attracted to their lightness. And whatever you call that *je ne sais quoi* (joy? energy? spark?) — you want some of it.

The "otherness" of such people is a direct result of their union with the Other. Deep interior work and letting go always manifest themselves in an exterior way. Like the anchor on the seabed, they begin to take some of the Earth's characteristics: steady, calm, dazzling. Even up on the surface, they are freer. They are not afraid of going under water, as they have an intimate familiarity with what lies beneath.

If union is authentic, it will "engender humility, love, death to self, simplicity, silence." Consider it your quick and easy spiritual self-assessment tool: how alive, spacious, and free am I?

Of course, while still on earth, none of us can be in perfect union with God all the time. In fact, according to the mystics, if a transformed soul were to constantly experience the intensity of divine union, he or she would die. We would be obliterated by Being. So instead, the person in union most often feels as if God were asleep. Upon waking, he finds us thirsty and open, and cannot help but unite himself mightily to us. Love leaps up like a "living flame" from the ever-burning hearth. We are ravished. To use the marriage analogy: what man can resist his wife who is supple and ready to receive him?

There are no words that can describe this union. Some mystics, after tasting God in this way, burned up all their previous writings. "It is all straw!", one purportedly said about his brilliant writings. When one experiences God so profoundly, pierced to the center of the soul, from whence one's breath originates— words fail. It is a dark knowing.

Bliss. Loved! My every cell is desired, touched, and delighted in.

Tenderness in a caress
Then: A gasp of hope —
— and there I hang, suspended in the gasp.
Breath —
Exquisite pain — oh, please, more!
Darkness
He is with me.
Known, into my very entrails
Love surrounds me like air
This is where I rest.

We dance around a dark and beautiful mystery.

Heaven

Heaven, the eternal afterlife, will be far from what we know in this lifetime. We have our hints: bliss; mirth; togetherness; belonging; being fully known, fully loved. But the mystics remind us that even these are only a shadow of what's to come. It will be as radically different as new life is to the just-born fetus. Sure, the fetus has hints of the life that is coming. Muffled sounds, brightness and darkness, the emotions of love or safety or fear. But what they know of their warm, secure, wet world can do little to prepare them for the life ahead. I imagine the transition is terrifying. Perhaps you sense the changes coming. Your position shifts and you realize this is not like anything you have ever experienced before. Suddenly spasms in your entire world begin to contract upon you. Confusion; pain; fear. And then — something gives. You are on the other side. You can hardly see: the light is blinding; the sounds abrasive, loud. You begin to use organs that you didn't know you had — or had never used fully. Your first breath of air. Sounds that once seemed a part of your world — a part of you! — are now coming from outside of you. A blur of colors whirls around you. After a shuffle, you feel warmth again. You sense a deeply familiar presence. Perhaps this place is Love.

·

Our minds cannot prepare us for the two big life transitions of birth and death. Our inklings are muffled and obscure, as sounds and colors are to a fetus in the womb. The shadows are only dark hints. "What would [this life] it be in comparison with the felicity which is promised in the life to come!"[90] John is convinced. As much as he sings of the exquisite delights of spiritual marriage, he reminds us: "A permanent actual union in this life is impossible; such a union can only be transient."[91] In heaven alone will we find true happiness. There will be the I-know-not-what that we long for.

But does this, then, imply that heavenly union will finally put a stop to our longings?

Surprisingly, the answer is no. If heaven is enjoying the life of the divine, it must be anything but static. Love always includes the ebb and flow of desire and fulfillment, *eros* and *agape*. In fact, if you step back and consider what it would feel like to be perfectly satisfied, doesn't it strike you as — well, disappointing? Instead of being a walking thirst, you are "content." No more desire. Look: you are holding your cup, hole in the bottom patched, and it is filled with water. "There! Now you have what you want, right?"

No. This will not do.

Instead, our thirst will continue to grow and continue to be quenched. For all eternity. Our longing is our spiritual lungs that we have never used — at least not fully. Our first breath of heaven's air will shock us into a vitality we have never known. Like newborn babies, we will learn and grow, with all of Infinity to explore. Our lungs will expand as we learn to breathe. And our breath will be the inhale and exhale of divine love.

"When we have found him, we go on searching because he is without bounds... He fills those who seek him, insofar as their capacity permits; and he increases the capacity in those who find him, so that they might again seek to be filled."

Conclusion

There is a reason for the ache.

"Hold on!" The mystics seem to call out from the other side of life. "It's coming. I promise."

We are made for union. We have wandered far from home, and sense that we do not belong in this alien place. Our longing is at once the map and the path. It guides us along the way; and is the way in which we must remain, even when uncomfortable.

The staying, the waiting, the longing, and the filling are all part of prayer. While our words and beads may help prepare us, the end game is far bigger. Tantalizing us with his delightful alluring, Love draws us into a dark union. It is his own inner life, his own Breath, that he draws us into. He longs… he receives. We long… we receive.

Waiting is painful. The I-know-not-what gently carves out more space within us, so we can fit even more delight. If we can trust that the pain of carving is also tenderness, we can recognize that our poverty is also our riches. The wealthiest man is the one who has the greatest capacity to receive.

Fortunately, the drama of prayer is led by the Spirit. He is the primary actor; his movements are already in us. He was the first to be moved by longing, and as he seeks union with you, he places his own desire within your soul. All we are asked to do is show up and enter into the place where he dwells. When we offer him the gift of our receptivity, "[He] does not delay, if we do not fail to hope."[92]

We are made for the I-do-not-know-what. The springs that do not run dry, the homecoming after exile, the union with the Beloved. While we get a real taste here below, the delight teases us. We cannot stand limitations when we were made for the infinite. But the wound that pains us also gives us our only hope: it is a promise of union. For in eternity, we will finally find what we are looking for. Rather than being satisfied, our longing will deepen. Instead of cursing the ache, we will beg for greater caverns, so that we can experience more of the life that is "always new and increasingly amazing."[93]

"So, my brothers, let us continue to desire, for we *shall* be filled."[94]

APPENDIX

Now What?

Practical tips for sitting in desire

So we know a bit about what this longing is and where it comes from. We know it is drawing us to a divine destiny. But what, dear companions on the journey, do we do with it in the meantime?

In the most practical part of the book, we will look at five strategies for living "in the meantime." Because that's where the real difficulty enters.

1. Be present to it.

My Netflix frequency is a pretty good indicator of how I'm doing internally. When something is amiss, a brainless, feel-good flick is part of my self-care routine. A few episodes of a lighthearted story—far removed from my present circumstances—is a fine numbing agent. Sometimes it provides just enough perspective to calm down, take the edge off, and explore what's underneath my "funk."

The real call is to be present to the beckoning. Sometimes, those calls are more sweet than bitter. For me, that is in nature. It beckons, but the silence is tender. Its arresting beauty demands a response as a grandmother demands you stay and eat your ice cream dessert. It is formidable, but filled with warmth.

Sometimes the beckonings are more heavily twinged with bitterness. These usually have to do with wounds, chinks in your armor where daily life hooks on and then drags like a dead weight. These are manifest more as anxiety, nervous energy, the inability to sit still or be silent, or feeling flat or numb. These are where our addictions emerge most powerfully. We will do anything to keep from feeling those negative emotions. If we let our guard down, there's no telling who will find a weakness in our defenses.

So instead, we drink, swipe, gossip, or give ourselves a shot of adrenaline by overextending and undercaring for ourselves. Meanwhile, the anxiety does not dissipate. Instead, the calling (yelling? crying?) only gets louder.

In truth, our emotions are telling us something. Something is seriously amiss. I hurt. I'm afraid. I feel out of control. If we can approach our emotional parts with curiosity, they are more likely to reveal their stories to us. The assistance of a skilled psychotherapist can be gold in this process. Often we have become so accustomed to our coping mechanisms that we've forgotten that we're coping.

The invitation: sit with your interior. Breathe. Be present to yourself and to the divine presence. If bitter feelings emerge, ask them what they'd like to share. How long have you been feeling this way? What are you trying to tell me? When is the first time you felt that way? If the experience is less bitter and more "existential" (you can often tell by the level of anxiety present in your body)—again, sit. Press in, gently. The longing will stretch itself, and make space for the gift that is coming. Trust that the divine is already present, waiting to pour himself into those depths. Make like John and beg that divine Lover to slay you. "Come already! I need you— come!"

He cannot withstand an open, receptive heart.

2. Clear out.

How do we make sure we are open? Do we even have space for the Spirit to come fill?

The process of clearing out is critical for any spiritual path. Withheld forgiveness, desperately unmet needs, and triggers from past hurts all can get in our way of exquisite happiness.

There are two important caveats here. One is that we do not need to be perfectly "whole" or "emptied out" in order to experience happiness. There is no need to fret or stress out that "I cannot get healed" or that the process is not happening quickly enough. Those pressures come from our inner critic, not our loving Center where the divine dwells. There is always room for happiness to grow, regardless of where we are on the path.

The second caveat is that God does the heavy lifting here. We show up, and offer up our availability. Again, strong-handing ourselves into healing and forgiveness is often counterproductive. The Energy that moves all things will also move our hearts when they are ready. He will give us precisely what is best for us in any given moment; nothing, more, nothing less.

Trust what is. Trust the timeline. Growth and healing cannot be rushed.

What you can do is begin to grow in self-knowledge, and ask for assistance in your exploration. Who have you not forgiven? Who would I avoid if I ran into them at the airport or grocery store? Do I have perfect ease in all of my relationships? A lack of forgiveness keeps us bound to the negative energy of a relationship, instead of letting it rest in the past. Where do I need to let go of hurt, or extend compassion to a hurting person? ("Hurt people hurt people," a wise person once said.) Where do I need to establish boundaries or perhaps close a relationship? And if I do move on, with what do I want to fill that available space?

(Image: God raising his hand. "Ooh! Pick me!")

Another piece to clear out is our unmet needs. We all have the need to be known, loved, and cared for. Other needs might include independence, adventure, attention, security, or solitude. If you have not already named your most important needs, put down this book and do so now. (There are tools on my website and other online resources to help with this brainstorming.) Why so important? If we do not recognize our needs and consciously fulfill them, we will find unconscious and erratic ways to do so. For example: if I have the need for attention, a conscious means might be to sing in the church choir every weekend, or ask a loved one to leave me a kind note a few mornings each week. An unconscious way might be throwing an adult tantrum when my spouse fails to recognize all my hard work, or spending extra time at the office in order to garner praise. When we have our needs met, we can go about living in a manner that feels free and open to possibility.

How might you meet yours?

The last major piece to clear out is unresolved issues from the past. This may include unmet needs and unforgiveness, but can also comprise much more. How do you know what your issues are? The tip of the iceberg are your daily triggers, or what a friend calls "disproportionate reactions to reality." Why does your micromanaging boss make you steam? What is it about your oldest child that makes you lose your marbles? Why does a certain behavior from your husband lead to you sulking and giving him the silent treatment? Our childish behaviors are a throwback to when we first experienced something similar.

Let me give an example. In my early twenties, I taught eighth grade for a year. It was one of those dif-ficult-but-awesome experiences, and thankfully I had a supportive faculty and staff to cheer me on. ("You know what the best part of your first year of teaching is?" A fellow teacher asked me. " — Your second year!") Unfortunately, my area of expertise, religion, was considered less important than the STEM courses pushed by the state. Understandable, you might say. However, when the principal asked me to include the anti-bullying curriculum in my classroom time, instead of during home room or any other subject— I was miffed. Trying to be rational, I presented my case. "Wouldn't this make more sense to include during home room time? They have twenty minutes and could easily split up the lesson plans for that. Other schools do it that way." Reasonable, right?

"Thank you for your input. However, it will be done during religion class."

I was no longer miffed. I was incensed.

This was all that I fumed about for weeks. How dare she! I mean, yes, of course she has the prerogative to make this decision— but how could she? It's *unjust*!

But as I listened to myself, and began to marvel about just how angry that made me— I could recognize that something deeper was going on here. When could I first remember feeling that way?

127

My older sister. Bossing me around. Pinning me under her thumb. No escape or way around. You had to do what she said. I was powerless. And I despised it.

Once identified, this experience was more understandable. I could address that past feeling of powerlessness and try to replace it with a script that was true. "I am not powerless. I can affect change. I have a choice. I can do what she says, or I could rebel and do what I want and deal with the consequences. I could leave the job entirely if I want. I have the power to choose."

What are your triggers? If you cannot identify four or five, enlist the help of loved ones. It is likely they can easily identify the top five (or ten) topics, situations, or people who cause a disproportionate response!

The other way to identify unresolved issues is through the process listed above: sitting in your emotions. Look them over with compassion and curiosity. As an experiment, try setting aside your habits or benign addictions for a week. Read a book before bed every night? Watch hours of TV? Always on the run from work to kids' events to volunteering to church? Flip through your phone during meals or downtime?

Pick a habit to temporarily suspend. Instead, use the time to explore your interior. What does it have to say?

3. Live Now.

Clearing out the "squatters" within is an important way to make room for the divine. Happiness needs some place to go! But what we don't want is navel-gazing. We don't want to become so fixated on our growth, healing, and self-improvement that we wallow in it and miss the present. "Now" is where life is happening, and where you will encounter Spirit.

Show up for life! The modern mindfulness movement is all about this. Eat when you are eating. Listen when you are listening. Work when you are working. It may be a trendy movement now, but spiritual traditions have been calling us to this since time began. The divine is pure Be-ing. All he does is "be", and allow everything else to be. How do we actively join in?

One important way of living now is through gratitude. Thankfulness draws our attention from past and future and reminds us of the goodness of today. What's your gratitude routine? I know people who journal their thanks every night, enter three items on their daily calendar, or started a family tradition of sharing one thing they're grateful for over dinner. Sometimes it's just needed as a reality check. When things start to spin out of control, gratitude is grounding. What is good about this present moment? How do I already have what I need for my current situation? What positive things can I focus on, instead of making neural ruts in the negative?

It is easy to forget that we have everything we need to live the present moment well. This does not always mean that it will be serene and perfectly measured. It may mean it is goofy, challenging, or downright uncomfortable. You might be in transition time, between jobs, relationships, or places in life. Trust that is where you are meant to be. You might be in a quandary, stuck between two goods ("People would kill for option A—but option B just seems to fit better. Am I crazy to turn down 'A'?"). Trust that when the decision is to be made, you'll know. Or, if it continues to be unclear, that either option will be blessed. Where is the divine inviting you in any given moment?

To hear it, we must live within our Center.

In my later teens and twenties, I had very practical ways of drawing myself into presence. At age seventeen, I began spending an hour a day in silent prayer. To draw that out throughout the day, I would write two or three words on my arm as a reminder of where I had begun. "Presence." "Wrapped up." "See the little things." I would notice these in calculus class and on the road home, and could gently draw myself back into that space. In college, having gotten over blue ink on my forearm, I would simply stop myself in my tracks across campus. Habitually, my to-do list would whir through my head. Stop at library. Call Heather. Finish paper. (Add about another 18 items.) — Then, physically stopping (and hopefully not tripping inattentive walkers), I would breathe, slow the hamster wheel, and take it off its fulcrum. I'd notice the trees, and how we were all sharing in the divine presence. After letting myself wander a bit interiorly, I could start again, this time hand in hand with the divine.

Being attentive to your breath is another great method for living now. Whether we are in physical or emotional pain, long, deep breaths can help focus our attention on Presence, rather than our difficult circumstances. I think of this as receiving Life with open palms. Instead of trying to grasp the pain and rebel against it — or even trying to grasp the beautiful moments so as to keep it forever! — we welcome what is. The acute pain of injury, illness, or childbirth are all

131

ameliorated by welcoming breaths. Longing, frustration with divine timing, and grief, too. Breathe in the Spirit, breathe out the discomfort. Sometimes this is all we can do to keep ourselves from squirming.

What are other ways that you ground yourself in the now? One of my favorites is tactile nature. It's not just "going outside", but being *in it*: lying in the grass, being part of the earth and field and sky. Perhaps I'll pick a flower or leaf or a smooth stone to hold while I walk. Something about its realness keeps my head from spinning off into oblivion. (I specialize in future thinking— comes with the territory of being a dreamer!) Brother rock and sister tree seem to do a much better job at *being* than I do. They live their mission and their rhythm exceedingly well. I have found them to be great teachers.

If you haven't yet found what works for you, peruse some of the literature on mindfulness. It takes some discipline, but gently drawing yourself to the present allows you to enjoy it that much more. And where are you going to meet Being but in be-ing?

4. Discover Your Authentic Spirituality.

If you had to distill your spirituality into five basic beliefs, what would they be? Try journaling this out: it may be harder than you think!

Many of us are wrapped up with preconceived notions of what spirituality should look like. Perhaps they are images from your childhood, or examples of heroes or saints or gurus you look up to. Perhaps you've found a new spiritual home in recent years, and are still trying to replace the idols.

Some questions you might consider in this process include:

- How does the divine move in your life?
- What are your most deeply held spiritual beliefs? List your top five. Hint: try reflecting on this organically, instead of writing down memorized answers.
- How would you describe the divine (I-know-not-what)? Where might your images need stretching?
- When do you feel most connected to the Spirit? (/God/Being/Jesus/Higher Power) How can you use that knowledge to adapt your spiritual practices?

- What is a spiritual practice that is attractive to you, but you've never tried in a regular way? I'm thinking silence, painting or sculpting, dancing on behalf of another, singing or listening to music, lectio divina, being in nature, mantras, or your own organic ritual. Where would you like to experiment?

- What does a good/spiritual/holy person look like? Make a list of what your current ideal is, without thinking about it too much. Try to list at least ten qualities, practices, etc. Which of those, if any, feel life-giving to you? Challenge yourself to eliminate or replace all of the ones that do not.

- If changing or eliminating practices feels scary to you, try speaking with a coach or spiritual director. What is the fear underneath that? If you were to experiment, what would that mean about you, about God, or about your beliefs?

- When do I bristle at others' beliefs or practices? Why?

- Where have I built walls that prevent myself from experiencing the love and freedom and bliss of the divine? What steps can I take to deconstruct, go around, or make a porthole in that wall?

- What role does my head, heart, and gut play in my spirituality? Which takes the lead? Which is asking for a greater voice?
- What are your top five values? How well do you live in accordance with them?
- Where is the invitation to accept myself more fully?
- In what ways do you share your spirituality with others? In which ways would you like to?

For those who have never done so, experimentation can sound terrifying. What if I color outside of the lines? Does this mean I am a terrible person, or that God won't love me, or that I'm betraying my religion? Am I regressing, or is this growth?

Trust your inklings. Follow where the divine seems to be drawing. There is no way you can mess this up. "Love God, and do as you please," Augustine advises. When love is leading, form matters little. When you are able to embrace your spirituality — the one that feels like the signature of your soul, perfect for the present (not your past or future desired state) — a vast spaciousness opens up. That is the stretching of our capacity, and the freedom of the Spirit. Now run along and play!

5. Live Lightly.

Lastly, laugh! Life is too short to take things seriously. Some of us melancholy folks forget that. Find joy! Suck the marrow from the bones of life. (Whatever that means to you— delicious foods, bosom friends, or crossing off items on your bucket list.) Love what you do and how you live. If you don't, take concrete steps to change that. Learn how to joke again (or for the first time!). Make laughter an easy and automatic response. Surround yourself with people who take themselves lightly. (I love G.K. Chesterton's adage: "Angels can fly because they can take themselves lightly.")

Pay attention to the little things in life. Take a small child for a walk and watch how they interact with the world. Kneel down to watch the caterpillar, or examine the intricacies of a spiderweb. Did you notice the perfect little droplets of dew outside, bejeweling the grass? I make a point of stopping in the parking lot each morning to take in the sky. In the morning I tend to be a fast-paced, let's-get-to-work kind of girl, so halting to simply notice helps me lighten my step instead of barging into work.

Rediscover your wonder, and that sparkle in your eye. We all knew how to once. And while there is suffering in the world and pain in the ache, that is not the whole of life. Devour the tantalizing tastes with gusto, like the happy fat man who knows the buffet is all-you-can-eat. Savor it! Try something new! There will always be more. You can trust that even if your preferred dish isn't on the table, it will be soon. Merriment is the greatest sign of trust.

What else helps you live in the space of desire? I would love to hear from you, and learn about your experiences of the ache.

I wish you a journey full of spaciousness, adventure, and heart-bursting joy.

About the Author

Kelly Deutsch is a Personal Growth Coach based out of South Dakota. She accompanies people on their interior journeys, to find new places of freedom, spaciousness, and vivacity. With a bit of spark and a real reverence, Kelly makes space for her clients to encounter their deepest selves, and there, to encounter the divine.

Kelly has degrees in theology and the humanities from Franciscan University of Steubenville, and pursued further studies in philosophy and theology at the Pontifical University of the Lateran. She received formation as a spiritual director while with a religious community for several years, and later received training as a personal coach through Coach University. With all that being said, she still considers her "alternative degrees" from sickness, silence, and solitude, to be her most important form of education.

She now resides in a delightful house nestled between fields and lakes in northeastern South Dakota. Her international roommates keep her chuckling, and her feline furball reminds her that it's sometimes more important to snuggle than to write.

If there's one thing Kelly cannot get enough of, it is the vast and ever-changing skies.

To find out more, visit www.kdcoaching.org.

Enjoy the book?

Please share it with others! If you're feeling kind, I'd deeply appreciate a review on Amazon. Your invitation may be the catalyst someone needs to embark on their own interior journey. It matters more than you may think!

Bibliography

Works of Augustine:

City of God
Confessions
Ennarrations on the Psalms
On the Greatness of the Soul
On the Holy Trinity
Homilies on the First Epistle of John
Letters
Reply to Faustus the Manichaean
Sermons
Tractates on the Gospel of John

Works of John of the Cross:

The Ascent of Mount Carmel
Ballads
Commentary Applied to Spiritual Things
Dark Night of the Soul
Letters
Living Flame of Love
Maxims on Love
Sayings
The Spiritual Canticle
Stanzas Concerning an Ecstasy
Stanzas of the Soul that Suffers with Longing to See God

Other Works:

The Constitution of the Order of St. Augustine.

von Balthasar, Hons Urs. *Theo-Drama, vol. 5: The Last Act.* San Francisco: Ignatius Press, 1998.

Benedict XVI. Audience 7 November 2012. Available online at: http://www.vatican.va/holy_father/benedict_xvi/audiences/2012/documents/hf_ben-xvi_aud_20121107_en.html. Accessed 10 May 2013.

_____. *Deus Caritas Est.*

_____. *Spe Salvi.*

Lopez, Antonio. "On Restlessness." *Communio* 34 (Summer 2007): 176-200.

Lewis, C.S. *Till We Have Faces.* Grand Rapids: Eerdmans, 1956.

_____. *The Weight of Glory.* Grand Rapids: Eerdmans,

1949.

Lindvall, Terry. "Joy & Sehnsucht: The Laughter & Longings of C.S. Lewis." *Mars Hill Review* 8 (Summer 1997): 25-38.

Matthew, Iain. *Impact of God*. London: Hodder and
        Stoughton, 1995.

Ogliari, Donato. *Gratia et Certamen: The Relationship
        Between Grace and Free Will in the Discussion of
        Augustine With the So-Called Semipelagians*.
        Leuven: Peeters, 2003.

Schindler, D.C. "Restlessness as an Image of God."
        Communio 34 (Summer 2007): 264-291.

West, Christopher. *Fill These Hearts: God, Sex, and the
        Universal Longing*. New York: Image, 2012.

Notes

1 *Confessions* 10.35.57.

2 *Confessions* 10.27.38.

3 John of the Cross, *Sayings* 15.

4 Augustine, *Homilies on the First Epistle of John* 4.6. Hereafter cited as *EpJohn*.

5 *Confessions* 8.11.27.

6 *Confessions* 3.4.7-8. Italics mine.

7 Proverbs 25:26.

8 *Confessions* 10.6.9.

9 C.S. Lewis, *The Weight of Glory* (Grand Rapids: Eerdmans, 1949), 45.

10 Pope Benedict XVI, *Spe Salvi*, 12.

11 *Letters* 130.2.3; 14.27.

12 Augustine: "We may go on speaking figuratively of honey, gold or wine – but whatever we say we cannot express the reality we are to receive. The name of that reality is God." *EpJohn* 4.6.

13 *Stanzas Concerning an Ecstasy* 1.

14 Prologue to *The Spiritual Canticle* 1. Hereafter cited as *Canticle*.

15 Cf. Prologue to *Canticle* 1, for example: "Who can describe in writing the understanding he gives to loving souls in whom he dwells? And who can express with words the experience he imparts to them? Who, finally, can explain the desires he gives them? Certainly, no one can! Not even they who receive these communications. As a result these persons let something of their experience overflow in figures, comparisons and similitudes, and from the abundance of their spirit pour out secrets and mysteries rather than rational explanations."

16 *Canticle* 11.

17 *Ibid.* 6.

18 *Ibid.* 27-28.

19 John of the Cross, *Commentary Applied to Spiritual Things* 1.

20 *Sermons* 103.1.

21 *Ennarations* 131.10: "Groaning is what wayfarers do, but praise is proper to those at last residing permanently in their homeland."

22 *Tractates on the Gospel of John* 40.10. Italics mine.

23 *City of God* 1.Pref.1.

24 *Ballads* 2.3-7.

25 *Ballads* 3.1-5; 4.1.

26 Augustine, *EpJohn* 4.6.

27 Augustine, *Ennarrations* 38.13.

28 Augustine, *Letters* 130.8.15, 17.

29 1 Thessalonians 5:17.

30 *Ennarrations* 38.13.

31 *Letters* 130.9.18.

32 *Ibid.* 130.10.19.

33 *Canticle* 1.8.

34 *Ibid.*

35 John of the Cross, *Living Flame of Love* 1. Hereafter cited as *Flame*.

36 *Flame* 1.13.

37 *Confessions* 3.6.11.

38 *Ibid.* 10.6.9.

39 *On the Holy Trinity* 8.7.11.

40 *Confessions* 10.27.38.

41 *Sermons* 102.2. See also John: "Enter within yourself and work in the presence of your Spouse, who is ever present loving you." *Maxims on Love*, 11.

42 *Confessions* 7.10.16.

43 Augustine, *Ennarrations* 42.9.

[44] *Confessions* 9.10.25.

[45] John of the Cross, *Night* II.11.7.

[46] Psalm 63:1.

[47] *The Ascent of Mount Carmel*, III.44.4. Hereafter cited as *Ascent*.

[48] *Canticle* 1.10. Italics mine.

[49] *Letters* 130.10.20.

[50] Augustine, *Sermons* 52, 6, 16.

[51] Iain Matthew, *Impact of God* (London: Hodder and Stoughton, 1995), 37. Hereafter cited as *Impact*.

[52] *Flame* 1.15.

[53] *Flame* 3.26: "And the desire for God is the preparation for union with him." See also Augustine in *Tractates on the first letter of John* 4.6: "The very act of desiring prepares you."

[54] Cf. *Impact*, 137.

[55] *Ascent* III.10.2. John's concept of *nada* loosely corresponds to Augustine's "desolation," though Augustine usually is referring to the bitter quality of longing in general (or rather, this earthly life), while John develops his ideas further, particularly in regards to spiritual growth.

[56] *Tractates on the Gospel of John* 40.10.

[57] This will be the work of heaven, as we shall see below.

[58] *Tractates on the Gospel of John* 40.10.

[59] *EpJohn* 4.6.

[60] *Letters* 130.8.17.

[61] *Ascent* II.4.6. See also Augustine, *Tractates on the Gospel of John* 40.10: Our longing must "expand to such a measure of capacity as to be fit to take in what eye hath not seen, nor ear heard, nor hath entered into the heart of man."

[62] *Impact*, 33.

[63] *Letters* 15, August 7, 1589.

[64] *Night* II.16.8.

[65] *Night* I.5.3.

[66] *Impact*, 78.

[67] *Ascent* I.13.11.

[68] *Flame* 3.18, 26.

[69] *Ibid.* 3.22.

[70] *Ibid.* 2.6. As the Spirit's desire to give – which is "great" – so "great will be the wound."

[71] *Ibid.* 1.23.

[72] *Letters* 130.15.28.

[73] Romans 8:25.

[74] *Confessions* 10.27.38.

[75] Luke 17:21.

[76] *Ibid.*

[77] *On the Greatness of the Soul*, 33.76; *Reply to Faustus the Manichaean*, 12.42.

[78] *On the Greatness of the Soul*, 33.76.

[79] *Canticle* 1.19.

[80] *Ibid.* 1.

[81] *Ibid.* 1.14, 18.

[82] *Night* 5. In his poetry, the soul is delighted with the night: "O night more lovely than the dawn! O night that has united the Lover with His beloved."

[83] *Stanzas of the Soul that Suffers with Longing to See God* 1.

[84] *Canticle* 9.3.

[85] *Ibid.* 9.6.

[86] *Ibid.* 9.7.

[87] *Ascent* II.7.8.

[88] Matthew 27:46.

[89] *Ascent* II.7.11.

[90] *Letters* 130.2.5.

91 *Ascent* II.5.2.
92 *Sayings* 26.
93 *Canticle* 14.8.
94 *EpJohn* 4.6.